apples

apples
a field guide

MICHAEL CLARK

Whittet Books
in association with
Brogdale Horticultural Trust

They went through night-time orchards carrying flares that lit lichened boughs and faces pale with cold. Toast soaked in cider was lifted on a stick to a little boy seated in a fork of a tree, a fiddle struck up and they sang:

Old Apple-tree, Old Apple-tree,
We wassail thee, hoping thou wilt bear,
For the Lord doth know where we shall be
When apples come another year,
So merry let us be . . .

They discharged a volley from their flintlocks to waken the god of the apple-tree from winter slumber and went back to the house and drank lamb's-wool from the wassail bowl so that, when they cheered 'Sir Pip and his Lady', their misted breath came to her smelling of ale and spices and roasted apples.
From *A Catch of Consequence* by Diana Norman (Harper Collins 2002)
by kind permission

Frontispiece: Barnack Beauty

First published 2003
Copyright ©2003 by Michael Clark

Whittet Books Ltd, Hill Farm, Stonham Rd, Cotton, Stowmarket, Suffolk IP14 4RQ

Cataloguing in Publication Data
A catalogue record for this title is available from the British Library

ISBN 1 873580 57 6

Photographs by the author unless otherwise stated. Many thanks to Brogdale Trust for pictures appearing on the following pages: 26, 29, 33, 37, 38, 39, 44, 46, 58, 64, 65, 68, 78, 80, 82, 83, 87, 88, 90, 95, 99, 100, 101, 103, 107, 108, 111, 117, 120, 121, 122, 124, 127, 131, 133, 134, 135 (Crown Copyright courtesy of Brogdale Horticultural Trust slide library); many thanks to Gerald Rose for the photograph on p.43 (and on the front of the book); many thanks to Frank P. Matthews for pictures on pages 49, 84,138 (2) and 139(2).

Printed in China

Contents

Foreword

What a splendid book this is, a rare treat, long overdue. The *Apples Field Guide* can be read at any level – what other subject has such intoxicating names, as alluring as the taste? Who was Tom Putt? What is the origin of Peasgood Nonsuch? Just look it up. Which varieties to cultivate locally and successfully, whether for cider, cooking or simply to pluck off the heavy-laden bower? How rare for something so enjoyable to be so healthy. In the process you may be helping to preserve an old variety, a national historical asset as valuable as bricks and mortar and at Brogdale we will almost certainly have every variety because it is the home to the greatest fruit collection in the world – another hidden treasure.

Michael Clark, who is himself Honorary Warden of a nationally important orchard, is generous in his acknowledgement of the work of others and hopefully future generations will be equally generous to him. He has made my job at Brogdale much easier and he deserves to have a variety named after him.

Peter Waine Chairman Brogdale Horticultural Trust
March 2003

Acknowledgments

My thanks go to all the staff at Brogdale who have helped with the preparation of this book named on p.173, and especially Margaret Burns for her help over the pictures and Peter Waine for his Foreword; to Diana Norman for allowing me to quote from her latest book; to Nick Dunn of Frank P. Matthews for kind advice and help with pictures; to Gerald and Elizabeth Rose for providing the picture of their Hitchin Pippin and hospitality on my visits; to R.M. and H. England for allowing us to photograph the apples in their orchards; to Angela and Martin Cook, Sheila and Michael Wadsworth, Margaret Armitage and many others for showing me their trees and orchards; to all colleagues in the Hertfordshire Orchard Initiative, especially its first Chairman, David Curry and Trevor Brennan, Susan Clark, Rachel Cottey, John Ely, Angela Forster, Martin Hicks and Dan Keech; Sheila Leitch of the Marcher Apple Network; for the long suffering support of my wife Anna and equally patient publisher Annabel Whittet; finally to Harry Baker, John Bultitude and Rosanne Sanders for their published sources of general reference and in memory of Robert Hogg and Thomas Rivers and their work on apples.

1

Why identify apples and preserve the old types?

OVER 6,000 NAMED VARIETIES of apple have been recorded in Britain and, although many are the same type with a different local title, there are over 2,000 distinctly different apples alone in the National Fruit Collection at the Brogdale Horticultural Trust in Kent.

Several years ago I asked Brogdale for grafts of all the apple cultivars local to the county to plant in the orchard where I live at Tewin in Hertfordshire. This is part of the Hertfordshire & Middlesex Wildlife Trust's continuing propagation programme on what is now a nature reserve. I should perhaps, at this stage, explain why I am so keen to promote orchards and the old varieties of fruit.

I was born next to the oldest farm orchard in Cuffley, south Hertfordshire. Records show that the farm already existed in 1429 and the orchard adjoining the farmhouse probably survived throughout its presence there, for some six hundred years or more. It was, however, built over in the 1960s and all traces were lost of the old building and orchard except for three ancient plum trees along our garden edge. I have never been able to identify the fruit which I call the 'Cuffley plums' and these are now reduced to growing on one tree plus a young tree I grafted in Tewin. As a child I saw my first juvenile hedgehogs when crawling under the border scrub in this orchard and the sense of loss as it was built over was considerable.

I was lucky enough to move with my family to live in the orchard at Tewin in 1969; the owner, Molly Hopkyns, had resisted pressure to sell the land for building. I have thus supported all the efforts of groups such as Common Ground, our Hertfordshire Orchard Initiative and local orchard groups elsewhere. Unfortunately, although Brogdale could provide nearly all the types from their collection, one of the Hertfordshire varieties, the Hitchin Pippin, was listed as 'false'. This meant that when the original two examples of each fruit variety came to their national collection (mostly from the RHS Gardens at Wisley in 1970), the Hitchin variety was mixed up, lost or later identified as something else. No other source of graft material was known and it was thought that this old English apple variety had been lost for all time.

I thought that the obvious place to put out appeals in the local press was in North Hertfordshire where the apple was described in two references: E. A. Bunyard's *A Handbook of Fruits: Apples and Pears* (1920) and H. V. Taylor's *The Apples of England* (1946). This resulted in very helpful responses, but of all the gardens I visited only one old tree in Hitchin seemed to answer the descriptions. There were no pictures published of the fruit and, due to its unknown origins, it appears to have missed illustration or a mention in the most famous book on apples, the *Hereford Pomona* (1876-1885). The research lacked that special source of reference in the national collection because at the time there were no other known named trees to compare with.

The Hitchin town tree was about 100 years old, in Angela and Martin Cook's garden on the south side of the town. Twice Brogdale had examples of Angela's apples to measure and examine, but on both occasions they were uncertain of the identity. The variety called Queen was suggested, but this is a cooking apple whilst the Hitchin Pippin was described as an early King of the Pippins dessert with a slightly dry flavour.

During one of David Curry's lectures on the work of the Hertfordshire Orchard Initiative, Sheila and Michael Wadsworth of Ickleford, a village near Hitchin, reported that they thought they might also have a Hitchin Pippin tree. I went to examine the fruit and was at last able to compare a similar dessert with the Cooks'. I found that fruit from both trees matched, although the latter tree was about 50 years old. Yet another tree, tall and probably over 80 years old, was reported near Weston, to the east of Hitchin. The fruit is like Charles Ross in external appearance, but ripens earlier and with a different flavour. Again the fruit matched.

At this time I described the apple on an early morning BBC Radio 4 country programme recorded from the orchard in Tewin. In Kent, Gerald Rose was listening and later telephoned me to say that when he and his wife Elizabeth bought their house 30 years ago the owner said, 'That fine old apple tree in the centre of the lawn is a Hitchin Pippin and it was in this garden when I was born here.' The man was no less than one of the Smith family who had orchards and nurseries in Kent for many years. An ancestor had introduced the Bramley to Kent.

So at last a *named* tree had been found. Gerald said that he had no idea it was of interest or rare and would bring the fruit up to show me. In trepidation I awaited the arrival of the apples in case they did not match our Hertfordshire ones, but they did. We have thus been able to save and propagate an apple tree which lives to a great age with delicious disease free dessert apples. It is now being presented to the national collection at Brogdale and will become available in nurseries again, probably for the first time in over 100 years.

You may well find the same loss of local varieties has occurred where you live. This book is intended to help identify apples, inform your choice of apple tree and encourage the planting of apple trees wherever there is space for them. They provide beauty in their tree shapes and blossom as well as food for us. There is also a surplus for wildlife which lives in and around their fruit and shade.

A significant date in the survival of our national fruit was October 21st, 1990, when Common Ground organised the first Apple Day in Covent Garden. The day became official National Apple Day thereafter and, like numerous others, we have celebrated this with events at Tewin Orchard following our first display of organic apples in the 1990 Covent Garden show. Scotts Nursery had a particularly attractive selection of apple types on display.

Although I was familiar with many apples from our own orchard and the comprehensive collections I had seen at Brogdale and the RHS orchards at Wisley in Surrey, it was difficult to identify the many fruit brought to our Apple Days for identification. The fruit from one tree can vary enormously and the vital background information on picking time, season, flavour and other characteristics is often lacking. Fruit from some of the local village garden orchards appeared over several years as we tried to sort out their true identity.

Visitors kindly bring named types for our displays and I now collect samples to show as well as sell on behalf of the Trust from Shenley Orchard in south Hertfordshire,

Blossom of Belle de Boskoop.

Elbourn Apples in Meldreth, near Royston, Hertfordshire, and Brogdale in Kent. Exhibitions are put on at local Apple Day events throughout Britain now and I have been very impressed with displays at The Marcher's Orchard Network in Hereford and at Brogdale.

The information on picking time, season and flavour is fundamental to the judgement of external appearance in the form of colour, shape, stalk length, and technical details. All the books I list can be a great help in taking your research on the different types further, but this Field Guide is intended to be complete in its own right without becoming too preoccupied with botanical terminology or lengthy descriptions. I include the most popular and successful apple varieties available and those you are most likely to find growing in your garden. There is a bewildering array of wonderful apples out there, but you stand a good chance of sorting out which is which, given enough information and this book.

It is a pity that the names of the fruit trees growing at a property are not listed by law in the deeds so that subsequent owners will have a plan of named trees. I list below the types found in our orchard, which was planted by William Stenning Hopkyns in 1931, as a useful indication of what were popular varieties then. Every age has its popular types and it is still possible to come across very old orchards or remnants of them. Over seventy years ago the pollination groups were well known and you can find particular varieties chosen for the timing of their blossom. If all your trees come into blossom at about the same time you stand a better chance of pollination and thus good cropping. The types were: Early Victoria, Grenadier, James Grieve, Worcester Pearmain, Ellison's Orange, Laxton's Superb, Cox's Orange Pippin, Bramley's Seedling, Monarch and Newton Wonder. They yielded about 80,000 apples each year from some 5,000 trees, 3,500 of which were set in cordons. Despite the extreme weather conditions of 1947, an exceptional 179,356 apples were harvested that year.

2
The Types

THE FOLLOWING FIELD GUIDE is arranged in eight groups: smooth-skinned, green cookers; smooth skinned, mostly green, sweet apples; striped, smooth-skinned sharp cooking apples; smooth-skinned, flushed or striped, eating apples; yellow skinned, mostly crisp or sharp apples; mainly red apples; reinettes and russets. Each group is organised in approximate order of general ripening date; its use indicated by 'dessert', 'cooker', 'cider' or 'dual purpose'. (I have adjusted the order in some cases to help contrast similar types.) The average seasons of picking and eating are indicated by the initial letters of each month: bold italic shows picking time and bold the season (the ideal time for eating). If the picking time and season are the same, only bold italic initials are shown. The following shows a fruit which is picked in October but not ready to be eaten until December and January: **J** F M A M J J A S O **N D**

Then size and shape of each apple type is given, followed by its flowering group and whether it is spur-bearing or tip-bearing (see pruning section, p.165). A spur-bearer produces fruit on short stubby shoots (the spurs) of two years old or more. These are the most common kind. The fruit on a tip-bearer is produced on the end of long shoots that were formed during the last season.

A number are famous as cider apples, too, and this is indicated. Cider apples are included in the list of named varieties from p.146 and there are several books devoted to cider production available, including the excellent recent study of the cider apples of Somerset, *A Somerset Pomona* by Liz Copas. Let us hope that the many other local varieties will receive similar treatment. The special taste and character of cider comes from these often very regional types of apple.

When picking a sample apple for identification purposes, try to choose one of a

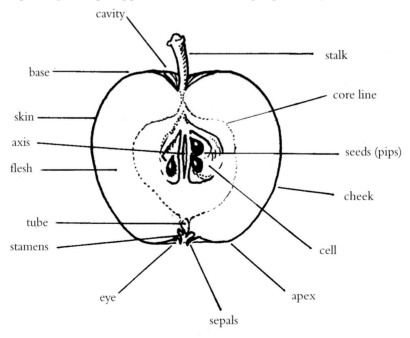

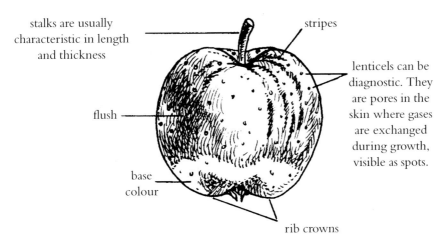

stalks are usually characteristic in length and thickness

stripes

lenticels can be diagnostic. They are pores in the skin where gases are exchanged during growth, visible as spots.

flush

base colour

rib crowns

What to look out for when identifying your apple.

typical size and colour when ripe on the best sunlit side of the tree. Information on ripening is vital in deciding if it can be accurately named, as well as the general flavour, cooking characteristics and keeping qualities of an apple. Note that picking time is not necessarily the same as the season; the ideal months for consumption are given with each variety. Early apples do not keep for long and late varieties may not be in season (i.e. ideal to eat) until a month after their picking month. Some apples keep right round to the following summer if stored in dark, frost-free, cool conditions, safe from small mammal and insect damage.

The text describes the known origins of the fruit and any variations in name. My own opinions of taste and texture are given, but taste is a very personal thing and you may disagree when you have tried different fruit yourself. Always check the ripening date and the readiness of the fruit to come away from the tree before picking. If you taste an apple too early it can seem raw and insipid; too late and it can be starting to soften and dry out.

The description includes features to help in identification. The following points are essential to identify the more difficult types: when they are ready to pick; when they are in season; how they differ when taken from different parts of the tree; the condition and age of the tree which will affect size and colour. An old tree with tangled branches and shaded by larger trees or buildings may produce very small fruit and become biennial in cropping (i.e. bear crops every other year).

Definition of sizes

Description	Diameter (mm)
Very small	44 and below
Small	45-54
Small medium	55-59
Medium	60-69
Medium large	70-74
Large	75-84
Very large	85 and above

IDENTIFICATION CHART

AUGUST

Early Victoria

Grenadier

Stark's Earliest

Discovery

Owen Thomas

Beauty of Bath

George Cave

Gladstone

Laxton's Early Crimson

SEPTEMBER

Lord Grosvenor

Duchess's Favourite

Devonshire Quarrenden

Merton Knave

Tydeman's Early

George Neal

Queen

Lady Sudeley

Keswick Codlin

Laxton's Epicure

Hitchin Pippin

James Grieve

Irish Peach

Gravenstein

Miller's Seedling

OCTOBER

Stirling Castle

Lord Derby

Warner's King

Tower of Glamis

Merton Beauty

Merton Charm

Katy

OCTOBER (cont)

Worcester Pearmain

Merton Worcester

Herring's Pippin

McIntosh Red

Gascoyne's Scarlet

Norfolk Royal

Mother

Emperor Alexander

Tom Putt

Cox's Pomona

Monarch

Wealthy

Bountiful

Peasgood Nonsuch

Charles Ross

Alkmene

Royal Jubilee

Norfolk Beauty

Harvey

Rev. W. Wilks

Greensleeves

Red Windsor

Winter Gem

Scrumptious

Laxton's Fortune

Ellison's Orange

Fiesta

Lord Lambourne

Autumn Pearmain

Sunset

Allington Pippin

Holstein

Lady Henniker

Saint Edmund's Pippin

Egremont Russet

NOVEMBER

Edward VII

Spartan

Gala

Jonathan

Belle de Pontoise

Bramley's Seedling

Dumelow's Seedling

Newton Wonder

Bismark

Crawley Beauty

Howgate Wonder

Lane's Prince Albert

Rival

Chivers Delight

Hambledon Deux Ans

Braeburn

Elstar

Golden Delicious

Arthur Turner

Crispin

Golden Noble

Red Falstaff

Kent

Cornish Aromatic

Jonagold

Idared

Mère de Ménage

Orleans Reinette

Blenheim Orange

Margil

Kidd's Orange Red

Cox's Orange Pippin

Jupiter

King of the Pippins

Ribston Pippin

NOVEMBER (cont)

Suntan 🍎

Laxton's Superb 🍎

Rosemary Russet 🍎

Bess Pool 🍎

Adam's Pearmain 🍎

Cornish Gillyflower 🍎

Princess 🍎

D'Arcy Spice 🍎

DECEMBER

Granny Smith 🍎

Encore 🍎

Annie Elizabeth 🍎

Wagener 🍎

John Standish 🍎

Red Delicious 🍎

William Crump 🍎

Pixie 🍎

Claygate Pearmain 🍎

Court Pendu Plat 🍎

Barnack Beauty 🍎

Lord Hindlip 🍎

Belle de Boskoop 🍎

Winston 🍎

Nonpareil 🍎

Ashmead's Kernel 🍎

Brownlees Russet 🍎

*Page numbers
for each type
are all listed
on p. 175*

JAN

Sturmer Pippin 🍎

Lord Burghley 🍎

Tydeman's Late Orange 🍎

Duke of Devonshire 🍎

Braeburn 🍎

The apples are listed in the months in which they usually ripen and their general shape and group is shown. Many of the later varieties have long keeping seasons and this is indicated in the field guide. Each group is shown in a different colour and shares common characteristics listed in the key below. Shape, colour and ripening times form the basis of the identification process. If you take or send your fruit to Brogdale, prepare a list of all the characteristics including blossom description, leaf type and flavour of the apples.

round	flat	conical	oblong	flat round	long conical

oblong conical	round conical

group 1: smooth-skinned, green and sharp (Lord Derby type) culinary apples
group 2: smooth-skinned, mostly green, sweet (Granny Smith type) dessert apples
group 3: striped, smooth-skinned, sharp (Lane's Prince Albert type) culinary apples
group 4: smooth-skinned, flushed or striped, sweet (James Grieve type) dessert apples
group 5: yellow-skinned (Golden Noble type) mostly sharp, some crisp and sweet dessert and culinary apples
group 6: mainly red, sweet (Worcester Pearmain type) mainly dessert apples
group 7: reinettes, skin coloured with some russet (Cox's Orange Pippin type) dessert apples
group 8: skin mainly russet (Egremont Russet type) dessert apples

GROUP 1
Early Victoria (Emneth Early)

cooking J F M A M J J **A S O** N D
medium round-conical/oblong-conical
flowering group 3 spur-bearing

Raised by William Lynn of Emneth, Cambridgeshire, it was first known as Emneth Early (1899). A cross between Lord Grosvenor and Keswick Codlin, it received the RHS Award of Merit and was marketed in Wisbech.

Like all early apples, they do not keep long. I have compared this popular garden apple with a rather 'later' early cooker, Grenadier, because both are found in many old gardens. Of the two I prefer Grenadier which is a more regular cropper, disease-free and superb with freshly picked blackberries, but both are ideal for summer blackberry and apple pies.

Look for a bright green, often small apple in unthinned or very old trees, speckled with grey-green lenticel spots. The skin is smooth and dry and there are obvious ribs. The stalk is thick and short, but extends beyond the cavity. The flesh is white, tinged with green, juicy and crisp. The blossom is ornamental and the leaves are quite large, oval, mid-green and quite downy underneath. There are always plenty of pips. (Whilst Grenadiers are still cropping well after 70 years at Tewin Orchard, the Victorias are long gone.) Can be picked in late July and may last into October. Its small fruit and tendency to biennial cropping lost it the commercial place it once enjoyed.

14

Grenadier

cooking J F M A M J J **A S O** N D
large round-conical/oblong conical
flowering group 3 freely spur-bearing

group 1

First described in 1862 by Bunyard, (Kent), but much older and possibly originally from elsewhere in UK. Commercial introduction was from 1875 and First Class RHS Certificate in 1883.

These disease-resistant and reliable cooking apples may not last long in storage, but are ideal in summer before the traditional 'keeping' culinary apples are ripe. My love of this apple in blackberry and apple pie is described on the opposite page, but anyone who cultivates apple trees will appreciate the value of such disease resistance, regular, heavy cropping and long life. If only all fruit types were so reliable.

Like all early apples, they do not keep very long (not beyond October) and are good part processed for frozen storage. They are a delight to core and slice before placing in plastic bags in a domestic freezer, and can be enjoyed direct from this stewed with other fruit. The flesh when cooked is sharp and pale cream in colour. Whilst on the subject of cooking apples, two favourites of mine are Monarch (p.28) and Mère de Ménage (p.88), although my overall preference is for the magnificent Bramley, (p.30), which is so juicy and disease-resistant, and crops, lasts and cooks so well.

Lord Grosvenor

cooking J F M A M J J **A S O** N D
medium large round-conical/conical
flowering group 3 spur-bearing

group 1

One of the prolific codlin group, possibly from Somerset (in Scott's catalogue, Merriott, 1873). Otherwise, its origin is unknown. 'Codlin' once applied to any immature green apple, but by the 16th century, Taylor explains, it mostly referred to the Kentish Codlin. The word derives from 'to coddle or parboil': boil until partially cooked, often before further cooking.

Introduced at the RHS 1883 Congress (the largest display of different apples ever staged) but superseded by Early Victoria and Grenadier. It is hardy and suitable for cultivation in the North. The old orchards may well have this variety because it was once very popular and widely grown commercially. Look for a bright green skin, which yellows, indistinct lenticel spots, in contrast to those on both Early Victoria and Grenadier, and distinct ribbing. The smooth, dry skin becomes very greasy in storage. Often lop-sided. The flesh is white, juicy and yellows as it cooks. An excellent tart flavour.

The blossom is ornamental and the leaves are oval, mid-green with regular, rather blunt serrations. They are only slightly downy underneath. George Neal ripens a little later and is also pale green, but has russeting and lacks the ribbing. They may both at times be angular, but George Neal has a more striking symmetrical conical shape. Be careful when picking and handling because they bruise easily, although this is true of all apples to a greater or lesser degree. More harm can often be done by novice picking and pouring fruit between containers than all the efforts of the weather or codling moths combined. We try to collect our eggs and apples with the same respect.

16

John Christie, a shopkeeper who grew apple trees in a garden behind his toy shop, raised this variety in Causet Head, and it was propagated commercially by Drummond of Stirling from 1831. A popular garden cooking apple and once used for quick crops between Bramley trees in Kent and then removed when the Bramleys had reached their full size. The trees have a weak, spreading growth, but it is a hardy Scottish apple which can be enjoyed as an eater by those who like a sharp taste. The best flavour develops in October. The skin is very smooth, but becomes greasy when stored. Flowers two days before Bramley. Look for the flat rounded ap-pearance of a small Bramley, but much more regular in shape and the blossom is very pale pink compared with the bright pink of the Bramley. Nor does the fruit develop the stripes you see on the ripened Bramley.

They are bright light green, becoming clear yellow, flushed orange brown, sometimes pink blotched. The lenticel spots show on the red, but are indistinct elsewhere. They have medium long, stout stalks. The flesh is white, very soft, juicy, acid and fruity. The leaves are medium size, mid-green with serrated edge. They slightly fold upwards and the underside is downy.

Lord Derby

cooking J F M A M J J A **S O** N D
large round - flat-round
flowering group 4 freely spur-bearing

group 1

This apple has been highly regarded since it was first raised in 1862 at Stockport, Cheshire, by B.W. Witham, possibly from Catshead (a large, old, angular English cooker known since the 17th century). It grows well in the north and is ahead of the Bramley, but needs thinning to achieve large specimens. There has been a commercial trade in these trees and they are often to be found in old garden collections. They are best sold bright green before the yellow pallor develops. The stalk is short, very fleshy and stout. The ornamental, late blossom reduces losses from frost, yet it crops heavily before the earlier flowerers. The flesh is white and cooks very well to give a mild, sharp taste.

The sunny side of the trees produces a pale brown hue, but the green persists until it yellows. The smooth skin will become a little greasy in storage and they do not last long after the turn of the year. They are successful where you have wet ground conditions, although no apples really thrive where there is waterlogging in winter or after prolonged, heavy rain. (I grow plums in such circumstances). They are very ribbed, with five distinct 'crowns' around the eye. The leaves are rather grey-green, pointed and serrated. They are very downy underneath.

Warner's King

cooking J F M A M J J A **S O N D**
very large flat-round-slightly conical
flowering group 2 freely spur-bearing triploid

group 1

From about 1790 this variety was known as King Apple, but it was re-named by Thomas Rivers from specimens given to him by Warner's Nursery, Gosforth, near Leeds. Hogg notes that it may have been from Maidstone, Kent. A vigorous and heavy cropping tree which is the first of our mid-season 'green' apples, and thought of as a good show and garden variety.

Often found in old orchards and easily confused with Bramley. The ornamental blossom is an important guide: it looks much the same in colour and size, but appears five days before, in the previous pollen group. The flesh is white, tinged green, juicy and brisk. It is more prone to disease than the Bramley, with problems of canker, scab and bitter pit, where small brown patches appear especially in storage and ruin the fruit. Like Bramley, it is triploid, needing two other pollinators.

The apples cook very well with a faint green tinge, but without the strength of flavour of Bramley. As a soft, fluffy and juicy stewed apple it is ideal with pork for first courses. Stored well, they keep to the end of the year, whilst Bramley can last until March or longer if the right conditions are maintained. Although the skin is initially dry, it becomes more greasy in storage. There is a red-brown bloom

and a little russeting, but it does not develop the strong dark red stripes of Bramley as it ripens and yellows, especially on the sunny side of the tree. Note the long, narrow, serrated and downy leaves.

Tower of Glamis

cooking **J F** M A M J J A S **O N D**
medium-large round-conical - oblong
flowering group 4 spur-bearing

 group 1

Old Scottish variety known prior to 1800, but its exact origins unclear. Hogg (1878) said it was common in the orchards of Clydesdale and the Carse of Gowrie (between Perth and Dundee). Although the apples lack the strong flavour of Golden Noble or Bramley, the trees can cope with the harsher weather conditions in the north. The juicy faintly green-white flesh cooks to a very pleasant crisp, but fluffy texture. A faint pear-like aroma is noticeable, especially when cut. The apple is bright green with a faint bloom. The base colour ripens to yellow-green. Look for pale green or russet lenticel dots over the slightly greasy, but smooth skin. Also check the leaves which are large and seem big in scale to the fruit. They are dark green and distinctly downy underneath. The blossom is mid-pink. The shape is generally symmetrical, but with angular sides and either four or five ribs which pinch in distinctly round the eye at the apex. This gives the same look an upholstery button can have when it pulls in material round it during sewing. There is a little russeting around the short stalk.

Edward VII

cooking **J F M A** M J J A S **O N D**
large round/ flat-round
flowering group 6 spur-bearing

group 1

Cultivated 1908 by Rowe of Worcester, Golden Noble crossed with Blenheim Orange. Like Golden Noble in colour, but keeps right round until April. It received the RHS Award for Merit in 1903. Not such a good cropper as the earlier cookers described, but the trees are disease resistant and do well in the north due to their late flowering and hardy nature. The apple's bright green pales to lemon yellow with maturity and they may show a distinct hair line or two down the side. The leaves are broad and oval, dark green with very downy undersides. Note the short to medium thick stalk. The lenticel dots appear as numerous little grey specks and there can be a faint pink-brown flush, as in the picture. The skin is smooth and non-greasy. A good apple for exhibitions due to the consistent symmetry.

The trees flower over a week after Bramley, but harvest at about the same time. Best used after November, when they cook to a pink hue with well textured white flesh. They have an excellent, rather sharp flavour. There has always been a commercial market for these apples; the tree is rather like Lane's Prince Albert in the garden: upright rather than spreading and therefore more economic with space.

GROUP 2
Granny Smith
dessert **J F M A** M J J A S **O** N **D**
medium round-conical
flowering group 3 spur-bearing

The story goes that Mrs Thomas Smith of Ryde, New South Wales, grew this tree in 1868 from chance seeds she threw out of French Crab and, although they are said to be unsuitable for cultivation in the colder climes of Europe, the initial RHS trials at Wisley (from 1935 to 1948) showed them to be good croppers here.

It is a famous imported dessert apple, but can be used as a cooker if grown in Britain. The blossom is a pale pink and the leaves are long, light green and bluntly serrated. The hard, juicy flesh is very refreshing and the fruit is the colour of bright green grass. This mellows to a green–yellow with some specimens flushed purple-brown.

There are no stripes, but the lenticel dots are very obviously speckled by faint pale green. The skin is smooth and greasy. The stalk is medium in length and the shape uniform, with some lop-sided, no doubt due to growing position on the tree branch. Taylor lists them as having a long stalk, and sums up accurately: 'A sharp, brisk dessert apple for March'.

Sturmer Pippin

dessert **J F M A** M J J A S O **N** D
medium round-conical-oblong conical
flowering group 3   very freely spur-bearing

group 2

This very late dessert apple from Suffolk formed the basis of the Australian and New Zealand fruit trades because it stored so well in export. Cultivated by a Mr Dillistone at Sturmer where he was a nurseryman, the type dates back to 1831.

According to Hogg, the fruit was the result of a cross between Nonpareil and Ribston Pippin and it has a distinctive, rich, aromatic flavour. The best of the crisp, juicy flavour comes with hot autumn weather. The flesh is white, tinged green.

Look for the exceptionally large pips as a guide to its identity. The original pip was planted about 1800. (The name 'pippin' refers to several varieties of dessert apple with rounded shapes, from the Old French *pepin,* of uncertain origin.) The base colour is bright green which yellows and the flush is a dull brick brown. There are virtually no stripes. The irregular shape, the crown and the overall green tinge to the colour are well illustrated in Bultitude.

The skin is dry and they keep very well in storage. The blossom is pale pink and ornamental in late spring. A good garden variety in a warm part of the plot. The leaves are mid-green, of medium size and thickness, bluntly serrated. They are slightly upward folding and very downy on the underside.

GROUP 3
George Neal

cooking J F M A M J J **A S O** N D
large round-conical/conical
flowering group 2 spur-bearing

Although cultivated by a Mrs Reeves in 1904, at Otford in Kent, the Neal Nursery at Wandsworth, London, put the fruit on the market in 1923 and it gained the RHS Award of Merit that year. Excellent late summer cooker, said by its high colour to be less popular commercially because this feature may suggest poor culinary qualities. When cooked it takes on a cream hue, is juicy and sweet, yet slightly acid. The skin is a little greasy, becoming more so after storage. The fruit can develop a distinct area of russet round the stalk and the eye, 'top and bottom'.

It is also worth checking the leaves on the tree to help confirm identification: they are rather downy underneath, fairly thick, and with rounded ends to the normally pointed tips of the serrated edges. They are rather smaller than the average leaf and tend to fold upwards slightly. The blossom is bright pink and they make attractive, spreading trees which crop well. They should be more popular, and although they are slightly later to ripen, match the season of Grenadier almost exactly.

Queen
cooking J F M A M J **A S O N D**
medium flat-rounded ribs
flowering group 3 produces spurs freely

group 3

Cultivated as a seedling (from pips of market apples) by a farmer, W. Bull, of Billericay, Essex, in 1858. Later marketed by the Saltmarsh Nursery of Chelmsford in 1880 and called The Claimant which, thankfully, became The Queen in the celebrations of the late Victorian years and now just Queen. Moderate vigour and good cropper of large fruit. Picked in August and cooked between mid September and December.

An attractive apple with distinct ribs and confused with Hitchin Pippin before the correct identification was confirmed. It is larger and a very brisk cooker compared with the sweet dessert qualities of the Pippin. Look for a very pale green ground colour which yellows and a variable flush, blotched with brownish red areas. There are also broken red stripes, but the lenticel spots are indistinct.

The skin is smooth and a little greasy in storage. The flesh is white, very sharp, soft, and cooks to a bright yellow hue. It is juicy and of good flavour. The stalk is medium length and the blossom is very pale pink, with mid-green leaves, broadly oval and bluntly serrated, very downy underneath.

Tom Putt

cooking - dual - cider J F M A M J J A **S O** N D
medium flat-round-round conical
flowering group 3 freely spur-bearing

group 3

An old type grown by Rev. Tom Putt, Rector of Trent, Somerset, in the late 1700s. (The reason I have headed this cooking - dual - cider is because although it is listed as a culinary apple, some people like the sharp tang as a dessert apple and it also makes a very successful cider, alone or blended. (Newton Wonder (p.32) is another cooker I have known visitors to eat from the tree with relish). A versatile, highly coloured apple which is vigorous, spreading and a heavy cropper. The apples range from the dull red striped and irregular ones to handsome bright red and yellow specimens. The lenticel dots are hidden but on redder apples show as white or red specks. The skin is smooth and dry, but greasy in storage and will wrinkle. The stalk is short and stout and the flesh is white, tinged with green, crisp, juicy and acid.

It has a bright pink blossom with large, broad dark green leaves, which are serrated, upward curling and downy underneath. There is a pleasant aroma to the fruit which has fairly large, plump pips.

Cox's Pomona

dual J F M A M J J A **S O N D**
large flat-round-round-conical
flowering group 4 spur-bearing

group 3

Although Bultitude considered it a cooker, this makes a crisp, refreshing dessert apple, too. Richard Cox certainly cultivated two remarkable fruits around 1825. Both this and the famous Orange Pippin were thought to be Ribston Pippin seedlings, in this case possibly crossed with the sharper Blenheim Orange. Both were from Colnbrook Lawn, Slough, Buckinghamshire.

It is an attractive garden tree with fair vigour, upright spreading. The distinct ribbing and flattened base are the best guide and the blossom is very pale pink, almost all white, compared with the bright pink of Charles Ross. They can be flattened on the sides and somewhat lop-sided, too. The flesh is white with a hint of cream and has a juicy, brisk, tang. When cooked, it turns bright yellow, holds together well, is slightly sweet and makes a particularly good baked apple.

Note how the pale green ground colour yellows with ripening, but remains green–yellow round the apex. There is an orange-red flush with broken red stripes. The skin is very smooth, but becomes greasy when stored. The stalk is variable: between short to medium and slender to stout. The leaves are mid to dark green, fairly flat and slightly undulating. The undersides are very downy.

Monarch

cooking **J** F M A M J J A **S O N D**
large round-conical-flat-round
flowering group 4 freely spur-bearing

 group 3

A cross in 1888 between Dumelow's Seedling (the soft texture of which it retains) and Peasgood's Nonsuch (which it resembles in shape). Where the bright red hue has comes from I cannot guess. Seen against our Bramley's it looks very red as it ripens and it is a sweet, 'first' cooker, before the Bramleys, that does not keep as well. It bruises easily if carelessly picked and becomes a soft, dessert by January. Introduced by the Seabrook Nursery, Essex, 1918.

It is the quality of the pinky-red against the lemon yellow which identifies it, although initially it has a pale green-yellow and bright red flush. There are a few broken red stripes and the lenticel spots are green dots. The stalk is short to medium and fairly stout. The skin is very smooth, but greasy in storage. The trees develop very angular beams, but do not reach the height and vigour of a Bramley. They are long-lived and a favourite apple of mine. The old standard Monarchs do not achieve the height or weight of old Bramleys, but are not far short.

The flesh is white and can be pink under the skin: an excellent flavour when cooked. The bright pink blossom is ornamental and the leaves are large, oval, dark green, bluntly serrated and slightly downy.

Belle de Pontoise

dual/cooking **J F M** A M J J A S **O N D**
very large round
flowering group 3 spur-bearing

group 3

Cultivated from an unknown cross with the dual purpose Alexander in 1869 at Pontoise, France. Introduced 1879, but remains an old type you may find in gardens rather than in old commercial orchards. Bultitude found it to be identical with Jeanne Hardy at Brogdale, Kent. It has the same purple red on yellow-green base as other varieties already discussed, but is much bigger and more like Mère de Ménage; it is also ideal for showing. Look for russeting around the long, slender stalk and lenticel dots which appear light on the red, but dark on the green. Brown mingles with the purple flush and there are red stripes.

The skin is very smooth and becomes greasy during storage. Can look orange at a distance. The flesh is white and soft and the flavour is worth trying as a dessert as well as in cooking. Some consider it only as a cooker. It has a firm, coarse texture, juicy and sharp, but without the impact of a Bramley, for example. Look for a very pale blossom, plump, large pips and a symmetrical fruit shape, although they are sometimes irregular. There are five ribs at the apex. The leaves, like the fruit, are large and serrated or broadly serrated, dark green and slightly downy underneath.

Bramley's Seedling
cooking **J F M** A M J J A S **O N D**
large-very large flat-round
flowering group 3 partial tip-bearing

 group 3

Cultivated by Mary Ann Brailsford in Southwell, Nottinghamshire, about 1810, this is the finest apple ever produced. Although its name cannot be changed now, I think 'Mary Ann's Seedling' would have sounded much better as a title, especially as she rather than the landowner deserves all the credit for its development. Flat and bright green until crimson flushes and stripes take over on a yellow background in maturity, it is best known as our favourite cooking apple. It is long-lived, largely disease-free, produces vigorous, heavy cropping trees with beautifully flavoured, juicy fruit. The apples stay on the trees despite autumn gales and if stored really well can nearly last until you are ready to pick early specimens of the new crop.

Apart from an understandable tendency to biennial cropping in old age, it is hard to think of anything harsh to say about such a remarkable tree. I even pick up late autumn windfalls and find they have lost their sharpness and can be enjoyed as a rather bland dessert apple. We press them with Laxton's Superb to make a sweet blend of juice, frozen in plastic bottles.

Dumelow's Seedling

cooking **J F M** A M J J A S **O N D**
large flat-rounded-oblong
flowering group 4 freely spur-bearing

group 3

Known in Leicester from about 1800, it was initially called Wellington. Keeps as long as Bramley and similar in looks, but not so flat. The size and shape is rather more like a pale Newton Wonder (p.32), and it is hardy. With a good flavour and heavy cropping from spreading, fairly vigorous trees, this has long been a popular cooker. Although they are less familiar now, you are likely to still encounter specimens in old gardens and some commercial orchards which once supplied the mincemeat trade. Look on the skin for well marked, russet lenticel dots surrounded by pale green. It is smooth, but there is a slight pitting and they become very greasy when stored.

The blossom is ornamental and copes well with late frosts. The leaves are a dark, grey-green, bluntly serrated and slightly upward folding. They are quite downy underneath. Although the apple's general appearance is green, they develop a bright orange-red on a more yellow background as they mature. Some broken red stripes and a short, thick stalk are characteristic. Pale cream in cooking and very juicy – more acid than Bramley or Golden Noble, for example. A good choice for colder sites where later flowering types such as Cox's Pomona and Encore are also growing.

Newton Wonder

cooking **J F M** A M J J A S **O N D**
very large   flat-round
flowering group 5   freely spur-bearing

 group 3

Although William Stenning Hopkyns had over 5,000 fruit trees planted at Tewin, Hertfordshire, when he established the orchard there in 1931, he reserved his cottage garden site for a Newton Wonder and it still stands there with long, rather sparse branches, and crops well. I first took it that the tree was named after Sir Isaac Newton's wonder at the laws of gravity, but I learnt later that it was found by a Mr Taylor, an innkeeper, at King's Newton, Melbourne, Derbyshire, about 1870. Introduced about 1887, it received the RHS First Class Certificate that year. The original tree lived for over seventy years. Probably a cross between Blenheim Orange and Dumelow's Seedling, it is a vigorous tree and the fruit ripens to bright yellow and dull-to-bright pillar-box red flush with short, broken red stripes. There are obvious pale lenticel spots. Look for the distinct roundness, although the apples can be lop-sided. I have known those who like brisk, juicy apples to pick these cookers off the tree and relish the refreshing flavour. Really a 'dual', therefore, to them. The flesh is creamy, tinged green and cooks very well.

The stalk is short and stout. They keep well into spring and can become greasy in storage. They have a strong pink blossom and mid-grey-green, large, oval, serrated leaves. They are fairly downy.

Bismarck

cooking J F M A M J J A **S** O N D
large round-conical
flowering group 2 partial tip-bearing

group 3

Sometimes spelt without a 'c', either from Tasmania's Bismarck or from the German Chancellor, and awarded an RHS First Class Certificate in Royal Jubilee Year, 1887; when the fruit is ripe it makes a picturesque tree. I photographed a tall specimen tree covered in fruit from top to bottom in Tony Hipwell's old orchard in St Albans, but it is just as successful in the north and crops heavily.

There is a distinct taper in the shape and the stalk shows much variety in both width and length. The pale yellow–green base colour becomes largely brilliant red, but it is not the Gascoyne scarlet:(p.80) the red covers more of the apple and there are fairly obvious red stripes. Look for light lenticel spots on the skin and a little russeting round at the stalk. Ribs show well at the apex as five bumps. The blossom is pale and the leaves broad, mid–green, with rounded serrations. Very downy underneath. Firm, fine textured pale green flesh which is sharp and juicy. A very popular cooker for its quality in process, when it turns bright yellow, and an excellent flavour. The shape is regular although it can be slightly flat–sided. The early flowering means it should be kept away from frost hollows.

33

Howgate Wonder

cooking **J F M** A M J J A S **O N D**
very large round-conical
flowering group 4　freely spur-bearing

 group 3

At our Apple Days these attract attention for their size and shape and sell at once. Here they grow near one of their parents, Newton Wonder, which was crossed with Blenheim Orange between 1915 and 1916, at Howgate Lane, Bembridge, in the Isle of Wight. Received the RHS Award of Merit in 1929 and introduced in 1932. They are also a brisk, juicy dessert and a useful blend in juices. Although the fruit lacks the character of the Bramley, it is pleasant baked with a good stuffing. An ideal garden variety for shows. It grows well in the north, but if shaded I find it susceptible to canker. Look for the very broad base to the fruit, which is flattened, and the short, stout stalk. The base colour is grassy-green which yellows as it ripens and the flush is a dull, purple-red. There are broken red stripes and traces of scarf skin (a thin, pale layer of skin mostly at the base of apples).

The surface is very smooth, dry and free from russet areas. There is a slight aroma when the apple is first cut. They polish up to look very shiny, but become greasy in storage. They are similar to Warner's King, but usually larger, more highly coloured and a little later. The blossom is paler. The leaves are broad, serrated, medium thick, slightly undulating and dark green. The underside is downy.

Lane's Prince Albert

cooking **J F M** A M J J A S **O N D**
large round-conical
flowering group 3 freely spur-bearing

group 3

Often called the 'Hertfordshire Bramley', this 1840 Berkhamsted apple was cultivated by Thomas Squire and received the RHS First Class Certificate when exhibited by H. Lane & Son in 1872. The more upright growth and lack of vigour when compared with the Bramley make it more suitable for smaller gardens. They do not achieve the size of fruit, either, but have an attractive bright shiny look and keep well into the next year if stored carefully. The grass–green hue is splashed with red stripes and the skin yellows. Sometimes there is no red marking. The flowers and leaves are very much like Bramley and appear at the same time.

The stalk is short and the shape of the fruit can be uneven. There is an almost circular cell around the pips. The white flesh, which has a hint of green, is very juicy and fine in texture. A very good cooker which keeps intact and retains a distinctly brisk flavour.

35

Encore

cooking **J F M A** M J J A S **O** N D
large to very large round-oblong
flowering group 4 spur-bearing

 group 3

Charles Ross, who has the great dessert apple named after him, cultivated this superb and attractive cooking apple in 1906. (I suspect the pun in the name was intended, but have never read of any reference to this.) It was awarded the RHS First Class Certificate in 1908 and shares with Edward VII the same picking time, the very late season and the same bright green colour, but can be much larger and can sport a large area of bright red–ochre and stripes. The lenticel spots show as either light dots or russet specks near the base. The stalk is short and wide. The main difference from Bramley is the more rounded shape, but the very high cooking quality is much the same.

The texture of the creamy white and very juicy flesh is rather thicker than Bramley. The blossom is large and deep pink. The leaves are light green, medium to large, with deep serrations and are very downy underneath. Like any of the late flowering types, these trees are suitable for areas which suffer from late frosts. As well as being one of the finest cooking apples, if stored carefully it will keep round to May and makes an attractive exhibition variety. Most often found in gardens, it has, however, been grown commercially to a limited extent in Britain.

Crawley Beauty

cooking **J F M** A M J J A S **O** N **D**
medium-small flat-round-round
flowering group 7 freely spur-bearing

group 3

Once known as Crawley Reinette and indistinguishable from Nouvelle France. It is also said to be an American variety, Goldhanger. However, a nurseryman, Mr Chead, found it in a cottage garden in Crawley, Sussex, about 1870 and the RHS gave it their Award of Merit in 1912. A long-keeping cooker which mellows by the following spring to be enjoyed as a dessert apple, too. Ideal for frost pockets because it has one of the latest flowering seasons. A fairly vigorous, spreading tree which crops well and suits the conditions in the north.

The shape is flat at the base and apex, lacking ribs. The stalk varies in length, but is quite stout. It is almost a miniature Bramley's Seedling in colour and shape, with similar long storage qualities. There is a grass-green base colour which yellows, flushed with brown-red and broken red stripes.

The lenticel spots are small and white and the skin is very smooth. It is slightly greasy and the flesh is white, tinged green. It has bright pink blossom with mid-green leaves, slightly upward folding, serrated and very downy underneath.

Annie Elizabeth

cooking **J F M A M J J A S O N D**
large round-oblong
flowering group 4 spur-bearing

 group 3

One of the longest keeping cookers and attractive in name, blossom and fruit. Its only drawback is a tendency to drop as it ripens. Thought to be from a Blenheim Orange with an unknown type, but Taylor also mentions Bess Pool, so these may be the parents. Cultivated by Samuel Greatorex at Knighton, Leicester, about 1857 (and still alive well over a hundred years later). Received RHS First Class Certificate 1868 and marketed after about 1898. The apple was given its name in memory of Samuel's daughter who died in 1866. Hardy, vigorous and suitable for all climates, note the heavy feel to the fruit, the roundness and the attractive hue. One very old garden specimen I know still crops well. The pale green base colour turns golden yellow with ripening. There is an orange-red flush with broken, bright red stripes.

The lenticel spots show up well as little grey russet speckles and the smooth skin becomes very greasy after long storage. The flesh is creamy, brisk and not very juicy. Cooks very well with a light flavour. The stalk is both short and stout. Ornamental bright pink blossom and dark, shiny green leaves. They are deeply serrated, upward folding and fairly downy underneath.

GROUP 4
Owen Thomas
dessert J F M A M J J **A S** O N
medium-small flat-round
flowering group 2 spur-bearing

Named after Queen Victoria's final Head Gardener, who was an expert on fruit, by the Laxton Nursery, Bedford, in 1897, which had crossed Cox's Orange Pippin with Gladstone. It was introduced in 1920. A spreading tree of moderate vigour ideal as an early garden variety to be eaten at once to enjoy the intense, rich flavour.

Look for the Gladstone (p.68) shape and early cropping from its one parent with the orange hue and excellent flavour of the other. The good keeping of the Cox has been lost, however, and the aroma disappears from the taste in a few days. The apples are flat-sided and often lop-sided, too, with five crowns at times on the apex. The colour is pale green at each end, fading to deep yellow centrally where broken orange stripes and red gathers, especially on the sunny side (see Bultitude's example). The lenticel speckling is indistinct, but can be found as little grey or green dots. The flesh is greenish white, and tastes sweet-sharp, soft, juicy with a good aroma.

The stalk is short and medium in width. The blossom is light pink and the mid blue-green leaves have a deeply serrated edging to look for. They are leathery, upward folding and downy on the underside.

Beauty of Bath

dessert J F M A M J J *A S* O N D
medium flat-round
flowering group 2 freely spur-bearing

 group 4

From Bailbrook near Bath, Avon, propagated by George Cooling's nursery in Bath in 1864. Awarded an RHS First Class Certificate in the Royal Jubilee Year of 1887. Book references mention the use of straw under these trees to catch the sudden falls of fruit on ripening for what used to be the main early apple in the markets. It is slow to bear fruit. I like the unusual flavour, but one friend thinks they are a disappointment whilst another recalls the taste from childhood as wonderful. (Apples always tasted better following childhood scrumping expeditions.) They are sharp at first and then sweet later. Best eaten in August, but continue into early September. The flesh is white, soft, with some red tinge, and very juicy. It has a yellow-green base colour with orange-brown flush and possibly the most speckled lenticel dots on any apple. The skin is slightly greasy, but strongly aromatic, and the medium-long stem is stout.

The blossom is pale pink and the leaves are medium to large, metallic blue-green, slightly upward folding and very downy underneath. There can be some fine-scaled russet on the apple which is of regular shape and they may have five crowned ribbing at the apex.

George Cave

dessert J F M A M J J **A** S O N D
medium - small round-conical
flowering group 2 spur-bearing

group 4

George Cave cultivated this fine Essex apple at Dovercourt, near the east coast at Harwich. After propagation, it was named and marketed by the Seabrook Nursery at Boreham, also in Essex, from 1945. A tree of moderate vigour, hardy and crops well. However, the fruit tends to drop quickly on ripening, like Beauty of Bath (opposite). It may be a cross between this variety and one of the Worcester crosses or with Worcester Pearmain itself. It colours brighter away from the UK, as I suppose we all do.

Note the yellow-green base colour, broken, rather mottled red and russet skin scars round the fairly deep stalk cavity. Large russet spots mark the lenticels and the skin is smooth and dry. It becomes a little greasy in storage. There are brighter coloured sports and the fruit was once grown commercially as a follow-on to Beauty of Bath. The flesh is white, fine textured, with a sweet-sharp, aromatic, juicy flavour. It has pale pink blossom and dark green, serrated leaves with very downy undersides.

Lady Sudeley

dessert J F M A M J J **A S** O N D
medium round-conical-oblong-conical
flowering group 4 tip-bearing

 group 4

This is a pretty red, striped, second early dessert cultivated about 1849 by a cottager, Mr Jacob of Petworth, Sussex, and was first known as Jacob's Strawberry. Lord Sudeley had it re-named after a striking red-striped Court dress worn by his wife when he was setting out a new orchard. It received the RHS Award of Merit in 1884 and was propagated by the nursery of George Bunyard & Co. in Kent in 1885. A garden and show variety and a good cropper, it also does well in garden pot culture on very dwarfing stock. In areas subject to late frost it is more hardy due to its late flowering. Look for a yellow-green base colour, later golden yellow, a bright orange-red flush over half or most of the fruit and long scarlet red stripes. Lenticel dots show as light grey russet.

It has a shorter stalk than Irish Peach, (overleaf), Stark's Earliest, (p.67) or Laxton's Epicure, (p.92), which look similar and ripen at about the same time. It has creamy flesh and a juicy, sweet, good flavour, but becomes sharp later. The blossom is orange-pink. The apples have many pips inside.

Hitchin Pippin

dessert J F M A M J J **A S O** N D
medium flat-round
flowering group 3 freely spur-bearing

group 4

Named after the North Hertfordshire town where just three trees have now been identified; there is no nursery or person associated with its cultivation. The only known *named* tree is over 100 years old and still producing good crops in Kent. The National Collection at Brogdale has two trees which are classified as 'false'. They have a superficial resemblance as they ripen, but do not mature fully to the colour or flavour. Graft material has been given to Brogdale and Wisley so that the national collections can include this important apple which was nearly lost (see pp.7-8). Identification came through appeals in the media. Bunyard described it as: 'A very nice fruit which may be described as an early King of the

Pippins.' The first record is in 1896 and John Aldridge has told me it was listed in King's Acre Nursery catalogue, Hereford, 1910-20.

Look for the ripe apple turning orange, with red stripes, like a flat Charles Ross (p.51); fairly regular, rounded, occasionally lop-sided. The stalks are short and knobbed. Lenticel dots show up as pale russet spots and the red spots and stripes are most distinct at the apex. The flesh is creamy, sweet, very juicy and with a pleasant flavour, described as 'dry' by Taylor. The bright pink blossom quickly pales. The leaves are mid-green, slightly up-curving. They are finely serrated and rather downy underneath.

Irish Peach

dessert J F M A M J J **A S** O N D
medium round-round-flat-conical
flowering group 2 tip-bearing

  group 4

Introduced in 1820, probably from Sligo, by John Darby of Addiscombe and Mr Robertson of Kilkenny. It has been a popular garden tree ever since. With its moderate vigour, it might have been a commercial success if its cropping had not been irregular. The spreading trees have something of a gaunt look, but when the fruit is picked and eaten at once they are superb. Take care to prune only when essential because it is tip-bearing: spurs are rare.

There is a pale green to yellow base colour on the fruit, flushed with a bright orange red. Streaking covers much of the apple and appears in a darker crimson.

The lenticel dots show up well either as a russet colour or white. Look for a short, stout stalk and a rather irregular round or round-conical, sometimes flattened shape, gently ribbed. Like all early apples, they do not keep long. The skin is smooth and a little greasy.

It has brighter pink blossom than Beauty of Bath, although the base colour of the ripe fruit is similar. The flesh is white, firm, juicy and crisp. There is a faint aroma to the excellent, well balanced flavour. The blue-green leaves are broad and bluntly serrated with very downy reverse sides.

James Grieve

dessert J F M A M J J A **S O** ND
medium round-conical-conical
flowering group 2 spur-bearing

group 4

James Grieve's Edinburgh apple has an uncertain origin and may have been open pollinated from Cox's Orange Pippin or Pott's Seedling, 1893. (It is a favourite of mine and the 70-year-old standards at Tewin have only recently ceased to crop well, at about 67 years). Awarded an RHS First Class Certificate in 1906.

It has been a commercial success, although easily bruised in picking, but much fewer are now produced in Europe and here. It is a regular and large cropper from vigorous, upright trees. If cut back as maidens, the trees spread out with age. The flavour is rather special and one that people who like fruit often recall with nostalgia if they have been unable to taste them for a long time. Look for a yellow-green base colour and broken orange-red stripes over much of the apple, depending on exposure to sunlight.

They have an excellent flavour, juicy, crisp and sweet. They can also be cooked in July, but will soften in storage when the taste becomes mellow as the smooth, greasy skin turns custard yellow. It is thus a very versatile apple. Lenticel spots show as grey-brown dots and the stalk is long and slender. It is slightly irregular in shape and ribbed, often lop-sided. There is a strong pink blossom and one of the darkest green leaves of all the apples, downy underneath.

45

Gravenstein
dual J F M A M J J **A S O N D**
medium large oblong
flowering group 1 fairly freely spur-bearing triploid

 group 4

The most popular apple in Norway and a hardy European type known in the 1600s. Various origins are given: it was probably from cuttings sent to Germany, at the Castle of Graefenstein, in Schleswig-Holstein from Italy where it was known as Ville Blanc. Recorded in Denmark by 1669 and came to Britain by the 1820s. Very early blossom. Too vigorous for the average garden, but a very juicy and brisk dessert apple, sweet-sharp, melting and aromatic. I have not cooked one yet, but some say it keeps its shape, others that it produces a fine juicy fluff. All agree that it is of excellent flavour in cooking and in Canada and North America it is commercially used for pies, sauces and juices. Look for the pronounced ribs round the apex and the often flat sides. The base is very flattened. The stalk is short and mostly within the cavity. The base colour is light green and ripens to a bright yellow with orange-red flush. There are short, broken red stripes (shown well in Bultitude).

The lenticel spots are pale green or grey dots and the pips seem small for the apple. The trees are triploid and therefore need two early flowering apple trees nearby. The blossom is very pale pink and the leaves are large, dark green, serrated and downy underneath.

Miller's Seedling

dessert J F M A M J J **A S** O N D
medium round-conical
flowering group 3 spur-bearing

group 4

Cultivated by James Miller, Newbury, Berkshire, in 1848 and given the RHS Award of Merit in 1906. Taylor noted: 'A variety of great fertility, which has been much grown in orchards to supply the markets with a low-priced eating apple.' Susceptible to bruising (see also Stark's Earliest, p.67), but a prolific early ripening and very pleasant eater. It tends to develop biennial cropping unless thinned and this will also increase fruit size. A fairly vigorous, upright tree. Note the long, slender stalk and slight ribbing to the apple. It is likely to be found in the older orchards. Look for a base hue of pale yellow-green, flushed bright red in part on a smooth, slightly greasy skin. There are short, broken red stripes and the lenticel spots become rather hidden.

The apples have a regular shape, often lop-sided and flattened on the sides, too. The flesh is white, sweet-sharp, melting, juicy and refreshing. There is a slight aroma. The blossom is light pink and the leaves are yellow-green, serrated and downy underneath. The pips are flattened and rounded.

Wealthy

dessert-dual J F M A M J A **S O N D**
medium round-flat-round
flowering group 3 spur and tip-bearer

 group 4

Cultivated by Peter Gideon, Excelsior, Minnesota, USA, in 1860. (The pips were sent to him from an open-pollinated Cherry Crab apple in Maine.) RHS Award of Merit, 1893. A very hardy apple (able to cope with the harsh Minnesota winters and named after Gideon's wife, Wealthy). Popular here for its looks rather than flavour. It makes an upright tree, with moderate vigour and good cropping. In fact the fruit is juicy and aromatic with a tang of strawberry. The flesh is white, sweet and soft. It also cooks well.

I have picked good crops from an old tree in our village for Apple Day and it sells on looks rather than taste, but it is disease free and keeps if carefully stored. Look for a pale green base colour and bright red flush with broad, deep red stripes which often enter the cavity around the slender, medium-length stalk. Does not over-crop and keeps a good size.

A likely tree to be found in orchards here from the 1920s and 1930s. Crops into old age. The shape is very regular and there are hints of well-rounded ribs. The blossom is bright pink with fairly thick, yellow-green leaves. These are slightly upward folding and serrated. The underside is a little downy.

Bountiful

cooking J F M A M J A **S O N** D
large round-round-conical
flowering group 3 freely spur-bearing diploid

group 4

Cultivated in 1964 at East Malling, Kent, from a novel cross between the cooker Lane's Prince Albert and the dessert, Cox's Orange Pippin. It looks like a pale Bramley, but is diploid, needing only one other pollinator. (The Bramley is triploid: requires two other trees for fertilization). They are also less vigorous and more suitable for small gardens.

After storage the sharpness of the fruit decreases and they can be eaten as a dessert. They have a creamy-white flesh tinged yellow, which is soft, juicy and aromatic. The sweet–sharp flavour is good and the slices just retain their shape in cooking. The skin is smooth and dry. Rather lop-sided, the apple's yellow–green base colour yellows with ripening. They later become about a quarter flushed with dull orange and scarlet stripes. The lenticel dots show up well as purple flecks surrounded by pale yellow.

The bright pink blossom is not quite as dark as its parent, Lane's Prince Albert, but the fruit looks like a 'Cox-yellow' version of Lane's. The leaves are pale green, medium size with shallow, rippled edging rather than deep serrations, upward folding and with very downy undersides.

Peasgood Nonsuch

cooking J F M A M J J A **S O N D**
large round-slightly flattened-conical
flowering group 3   freely spur-bearing

 group 4

Although thought of a cooker, this is a brisk and juicy dessert apple too and Bunyard considered it one of the most beautiful fruits grown. Cultivated by a Mrs Peasgood in the 1850s, when she lived in Grantham, she took the tree with her after her move to Stamford, Lincolnshire. Thought to have been a cross with Catshead. Thomas Laxton introduced the fruit at Stamford and London in 1872 where it received the RHS First Class Certificate. The trees are moderately vigorous and ideal for gardens, but may be susceptible to canker in places. You should therefore avoid planting these on the site of a previous apple. They can be mistaken for Charles Ross in the very conical specimens, but they have more russet flecking and the blossom is paler.

They slice up well in salads to give a brisk, refreshing flavour. The flesh is white, tinged green and becomes creamy. They are slightly sweet and tender.

Look for a pale green–yellow apple, turning lemon yellow with ripening, with orange-red flush. There are broad, broken red stripes and the lenticels are obvious as pale brown spots. The stalk is short and quite stout, often with a fleshy lump. The leaves are larger than Charles Ross, but very similar in their yellow-green colour and both are slightly downy on the undersides.

Charles Ross
dual J F M A M J J A **S O N D**
large round-conical
flowering group 3 very freely spur-bearing

group 4

Popular since it was cultivated by Charles Ross at a Captain Carstair's garden, Welford Park in Berkshire, and introduced in 1899, it was given the RHS Award of Merit and First Class Certificate in that year. Does well in Scotland, but grows in all districts with success and tolerates pure chalk soils.

Like a late Hitchin Pippin and a large Cox's Orange Pippin, the shape varies between regular conical to lop-sided broad and it lacks the distinct ribbing and five corrugated crown of Cox's Pomona. Look for a green-yellow base colour and orange-red flush with broken crimson stripes. Lenticel spots show well as russet dots and the skin is smooth, becoming greasy with storage. The flesh is a creamy white, sweet, juicy, firm and aromatic. If kept a long time the texture becomes rather soft and woolly. They are best used for cooking when still early in the season.

The stalk is short to medium and stout. There is very bright pink blossom and the leaves are medium size, yellow-green, slightly upward folding. They are undulating to the touch and faintly downy.

Rival

dual J F M A M J J A **S O N D**
medium-large flat-round
flowering group 3 spur-bearing

 group 4

Cultivated by Charles Ross by crossing Cox's Orange Pippin with Peasgood's Nonsuch in Newbury, Berkshire, from 1900, and given the RHS Award of Merit that year. A fairly hardy and wet tolerant dual purpose tree which was a commercial success in its day and popular in old orchards. The tendency for the big crops to become biennial probably lost it a prime place in the late market, and the crisp, juicy flavour is not as strong as its Cox parent. Look for a bright, pale green, ripening to yellow and orange-red flush to the smooth, dry skin. They become a little greasy when stored. Taylor saw it primarily as a des-sert apple, but the firm creamy white flesh has a light, pleasant sharp charac-ter when cooked.

Note the very short stalk which is stout, but sunk well within the cavity. There are numerous broken red stripes on the skin which can looked faintly hammered on the surface, and a trace of ribs. The lenticel spots are inconspicu-ous pale flecks. The blossom is mid-pink and the leaves are mid-green, bluntly serrated and very downy on the under-side. They tolerate very cold winters and because of their symmetry and colour are useful for exhibition at shows from the garden. There is virtually no aroma.

Chivers Delight

dessert **J** F M A M J J A S **O N** D
medium flat-round-round
flowering group 4 freely spur-bearing

group 4

Although prone to canker, this is a high cropping and long lasting dessert apple which stays juicy into the new year. Cultivated in 1936 by John Chivers at his farm in Histon, Cambridgeshire, it was marketed in 1966. From my experience it would be best to plant these away from where apples have been grown before to reduce the risk of disease. Although the parentage is not recorded, an attractive Cox-like appearance and the very long stalk are the characteristics to look for.

The flesh is creamy-white, with a crisp, honeyed flavour: a pleasant balance between sweet and sharp. The skin is dry, with a base colour of green ripening to golden yellow. It has an orange-red flush with scattered, broken red stripes. A few russet patches may show and the lenticel dots appear as large russet spots. The fruit is fairly round, but sometimes lop-sided. There is usually quite an obvious break between the flush and the base colour. The blossom is a strong pink and there are large, oval leaves. These are sharply serrated, downward hanging and grey-green. They are thin and very downy underneath.

53

Hambledon Deux Ans

dual **J F M A** M J J A **S** O N D
large round-conical-slightly oblong
flowering group 3 spur-bearing

 group 4

Found in Hambledon, Hampshire, about 1750 and may turn up in old orchards in the southern counties, especially around Sussex and Hampshire. In the 19th century it was said to be present in most of the local gardens here. A very vigorous, upright, spreading tree that crops well, but does not compete with Newton Wonder, for example. Prone to bitter pit and only fair in flavour, it does keep very well and is pleasantly sweet-sharp. Rather lacking in juice, the flesh is creamy, dry and tinged yellow. There is a slight aroma.

Look for a rather lop-sided, flattened shape, little or no trace of ribs, somewhat flat-sides and bumps. The base colour has a silver-green hue, ripening to golden orange, and there is a red flush. Most lack the reddening. There is faint russeting. Note the scarf skin (light layer around the stalk) and indistinct lenticel flecking. The stalk is short and stout, the blossom bright pink and the leaves are large, dark green, serrated and upward folding. The undersides are downy.

Wagener

dessert, cider **J F M A** M J J A S **O** N D
medium-large flat-round
flowering group 3 spur-bearing

group 4

Although this is an excellent late American dessert apple, it also cooks well and makes a good juice or cider. Can be used as a culinary apple early in the season, but will keep, and improve, as a dessert, round to the following spring. It was cultivated in 1791 by George Wheeler at Penn Yan, New York. His nursery was bought by Abraham Wagener in 1796 and in 1847 the apple was exhibited at the New York Agricultural Society. In 1883, Thomas Rivers brought it to Britain to be introduced at the RHS's great apple Congress in London and in 1910 it received the RHS Award of Merit. As well as being tolerant of late frosts, it is said to improve, like the sloe berry, after the first autumn frosts. The creamy white flesh is firm, crisp and quite sweet. Note the usually long, rather slender stalk and hammered, dry skin. This is grass-green but turns pale yellow and the flush is pinky-red with indistinct bright, broken red stripes.

The skin is tough, like several late-keeping varieties. The pale lenticel dots do not show up well and the fruit shape is rather lop-sided and irregular. The blossom is pale pink and the serrated leaves are bright grass-green. They are only slightly downy underneath.

Jonagold
dessert, cider **J F** M A M J J A S **O N D**
large round
flowering group 4 very free spur-bearing triploid

 group 4

The clue to the cross is in the name: a match of two heavy cropping types of apple in New York between Jonathan and Golden Delicious which has improved the Golden Delicious flavour and is exploited commercially in much of the world. Cultivated in 1943, it was in fruit by 1953 and introduced in 1968. It received the RHS Award of Merit in 1987. Good for cooking and cider, too. In this country it does not colour so well and the red sport is a better choice. Like many triploid trees it is prolific, but needs two other pollinators in flower at the same time for success. Although it is in season from November, I enjoy the juicy crispness of the fruit picked in mid-October. Look for the long, strong stalk, curving to one side, in contrast to the similar coloured large fruit described. The bright yellow base colour is tinged with green and the flush is warm to strong red. There are broken red stripes and small, pale lenticel spots. Note the thin russet round the stalk.

The skin is dry and bumpy. The creamy-white flesh has a sweet-sharp, honeyed aroma. The blossom is bright pink and the tree has light, upturning, sharply serrated, downy, grey-green leaves.

GROUP 5
Keswick Codlin
cooking J F M A M J J *A S* O N D
medium-large round-conical /oblong
flowering group 2 spur-bearing

Recorded in 1793 to have been found amongst refuse in a waste area at Gleaston Castle, near Ulverston, Lancashire. It was introduced by John Sander, a Keswick nurseryman in Cumbria and it became one of the favourite Victorian cooking apples, especially celebrated for its jelly to serve with meat dishes.

The trees are upright-spreading and crop heavily, although this can become a biennial event. Grows well in the north where it is still popular. The very ornamental blossom has always been appreciated in gardens and although the fruit is rather angular and lop-sided, the base hue is light green, ripening to pale yellow with distinct russet lenticel dots. Pale purple brown can flush some on the sunny side of the tree and the stalk is very short and stout. Distinctly ribbed. The flesh is light cream, tinged green, juicy and brisk. It is considered a dual-purpose apple by those who like a sharp, tangy dessert, but by tradition it is a cooker. The smooth skin can become greasy in storage. The grey-green leaves are small, pointed and serrated. The undersides are very downy.

Harvey

cooking J F M A M J J A **S O N D**
large oblong-conical
flowering group 4 partial tip-bearer

 group 5

Probably our oldest named cooking apple and from East Anglia. Thought to have been raised in Norfolk in 1629 by a Mr Parkinson, it was named after a local benefactor, Dr Gabriel Harvey, Master of Trinity Hall, Cambridge. Known from Norwich and London markets in the 19th Century as one of the most popular fruits. Although it continued in popularity into the middle of the last century, it is no longer grown commercially and is now a garden variety. Likely to be in old orchards and similar to Arthur Turner (which is more angular and has deep pink blossom), Peasgood Nonsuch (which lacks any ribs) and other large pale green mid-season culinary types. Look for an absence of red stripes on a pale green base which turns to golden yellow with ripening. The flush is red-ochre brown and there are often patches of grey-brown russet, on one side only. Lenticel spots are brown or green.

They are slightly greasy if stored. The stalk is short or medium within a flattened cavity at the apex. It crops well with creamy-white flesh, tinged yellow. It is a firm, sweet, good cooker with a flat-sided look and well-rounded ribs. The blossom is pale pink and the leaves are medium to small, bluntly serrated and grey-green. They are a little downy underneath.

Reverend W. Wilks

cooking J F M A M J J A **SO** N D
very large round-conical-conical
flowering group 2 very free spur-bearing

group 5

Like Sturmer Pippin (p.23), this apple was a Ribston Pippin cross, but in this case with Peasgood's Nonsuch and the result is in complete contrast: it is early ripening and has no keeping qualities. It was cultivated by J. Allgrove, manager of Veitch's Nursery, near Slough, Buckinghamshire. It received the RHS Award of Merit in 1904 and their First Class Certificate in 1910. It was named after a highly regarded RHS secretary, the vicar of Shirley Parish, South London (who raised the first Shirley Poppies).

They grow to a compact size and have an ornamental, bright pink blossom. This makes them an ideal garden and show variety with the fruit large, or very large in display. It crops well and quite early, but can become biennial. It is best to thin the growing apples to reduce this trait. Look for a very pale creamy-white base colour, flushed with a mottled pale orange. There are a few broken red stripes and the lenticel spots show up as small green russet speckling.

The skin is dry, but becomes greasy in storage. The stalk is short and slender. It does not extend beyond the fruit cavity. The flesh is very white, crisp, sweet, juicy and yellows in cooking. The leaves are dark green, oval, serrated and slightly upward folding. The undersides are slightly downy.

Greensleeves

dessert, cider J F M A M J J A *S O* N D
medium round-oblong
flowering group 3 partial tip-bearer

 group 5

A 1966 cross made by Dr F. Alston at East Malling in Kent of James Grieve and Golden Delicious. Because it was raised under forty years ago, it will not feature in any of the very old orchards and is more likely to be on dwarfing rootstock in gardens.

They are quick to come into bearing and prolific. The pale green becomes yellow, much as those from a James Grieve tree change to custard yellow with maturity. The hue is like its other 'parent', Golden Delicious. The skin is smooth and there may be some russeting in the stalk cavity. It has a thin, elongated stalk. Makes a good cider and juice.

There is a very refreshing and crisp taste to the creamy white flesh. When eaten early in the season it is hard and sharp but with age it becomes softer and sweeter. With such a good pedigree we would expect a special apple and apart from the rather tough skin and the way the flavour does trail off quite quickly, it is crunchy with a good tang. Many people are 'snooty' about Golden Delicious, but see my comments on this American apple when English grown and allowed to ripen (opposite). The blossom is ornamental and the light green leaves are bluntly serrated. They are not very downy. The fruit is best eaten in the first two months of its season rather than in November.

Golden Delicious

dessert **J F** M A M J J A S **O N D**
medium round-conical-oblong
flowering group 4 very freely spur-bearing

group 5

Unfairly maligned from the supermarket specimens imported unripe and rather tasteless as a result, this 1890 American apple needs warmth to do well and when grown against a south facing wall in Britain, it is superb, enjoyed straight from the tree around late October or early November. Like the other initially green apples in this group, it becomes bright yellow when mature and shows numerous easily recognised brown russet lenticel spots across smooth, non–greasy skin. The fairly vigorous trees produce regular full crops of fruit which need to be thinned to retain a large size in this country. Introduced here in 1914 by Stark Brothers, it is likely to be found in many garden orchards.

The fruit has five crowns at the apex and clear ribbing as it tapers downwards. Look for the long pale and sharply serrated green leaves on the tree with faint down on the underside. The fruit is 'tall' and the stalk is noticeably long. A tree–ripened fruit picked as I describe above is full of flavour with a crisp, sweet and juicy texture.

Arthur Turner

cooking J F M A M J J A **S O** N D
large round-conical-slightly oblong
flowering group 3 freely spur-bearing

 group 5

An ornamental flowering, early cooker which Charles Turner cultivated at Slough, Buckinghamshire, in 1912 when it was first known as Turner's Prolific. Certainly a good cropper, it received the RHS Award of Merit that year and was re-named Arthur Turner in 1913. It is a vigorous and upright tree. They are resistant to scab and grow well in the north. Never widely grown commercially, although it can be picked early, like Grenadier, and used ahead of Bramley. It takes longer than many to cook, but it yellows to a brisk, pleasant pulp. Look for a pale green base colour which yellows in patches as it ripens and a variable pink or purple-brown flush without stripes. The surface is very smooth and dry, speckled with a thin grey russet. The fine white lenticel spots are not obvious.

Note the very short stalk sunk in the cavity. The flesh is creamy-white under a tough skin, which gives an excellent early pie, baked apple or sauce. The leaves are large and broadly oval. They are bluntly serrated, medium thick, slightly upward-folding, mid green and very downy underneath.

62

Norfolk Beauty

cooking J F M A M J J A **S O N D**
large round - round-conical
flowering type 2 partial tip-bearer

group 5

Cultivated in Gunton Park, Norwich, 1901, by a Mr Allan. Probably Warner's King crossed with Waltham Abbey, it received an RHS First Class Certificate in 1902. A vigorous, spreading and hardy mid-season cooker, able to cope with the chill east coast winds in winter. Although the colour is like Arthur Turner, opposite, some can develop a large area of pink or purple-brown blush, especially on the sunny side of the tree. Like Lord Derby and Royal Jubilee it yellows with maturity from a bright green. There are patches of russet top and bottom, but the skin is generally dry and smooth except where the russet creates a little roughness. The flesh is creamy, sweet-sharp and, when cooked, breaks up as stewed apple rather than fluffing up with the process.

The blossom is mid-pink and the leaves are sharply serrated, blue-green, quite large and downy underneath. When you regard the shape of the fruit in identification you find good symmetry and, apart from those flushed from the extra light on one side, even colour. There is a brown russet area in the cavity around the stalk. The stalk is usually short and level with the base. The little spots which allow the fruit to 'breathe', the lenticels, are obvious in places as russet or green ringed dots.

63

Crispin
dual, cider **J F** M A M J J A S **O N D**
large oblong
flowering group 3 freely spur-bearing triploid

group 5

A Japanese variety from 1930, it received the RHS Award of Merit in 1970. Known world-wide as Mutsu, it was given an English name when marketed here.

With five distinct crown at the apex, the fruit looks very angular and is large if thinned well. It tends to become a biennial cropper, but, with attention, crops heavily and regularly. A good commercial type which has virtually no russeting except in the spotting around the lenticels. A reddish bloom can show on the otherwise light green, which pales to more of a yellow hue with maturity. The skin is dry and the stalk extends well beyond the fruit. The blossom is showy and ornamental. The leaves are large, too, and deeply serrated without much down on the underside.

There is a faint green tinge to the white flesh and although the flavour is not strong, it is pleasant, with good texture. It does not need much sugar when cooked because it is naturally sweet-sharp and juicy in taste.

I can vouch for the excellent light cider it makes, too. Like Bramley, pollination is triploid, needing at least two other sources of pollen for good fertilization. Keeps into the new year if stored well.

Royal Jubilee

cooking J F M A M J J A **S O N D**
medium oblong-conical
flowering group 5   freely spur-bearing

group 5

Recorded in 1888 from Hounslow, Middlesex, and put on the market by Bunyard at Maidstone in Kent. The green is tinged with yellow and this turns into a fairly uniform lemon with a purple flush in some. The fruit tend to fall at about the same time and can catch you out: pick in September as soon as they come away in your hand. They are not considered to be very attractive apples, but I find the shape and colour appealing and they crop regularly and in good quantities from rather weak, spreading trees. The leaves are worth checking if you have difficulty in the identification of this apple: they are distinctly downward turning (unlike the usual apple leaf that curves upwards). They are also very downy underneath.

The blossom is ornamental pink and, being late, frost resistant. The skin is smooth and slightly greasy. In storage they become much more so. Cut open, they show a large cell around the seeds. Do not expect a strong flavour, but they remain intact with a cream colour when cooked. There is a pear-like taste and they make a good juice.

Golden Noble

cooking J F M A M J J A S **O N D**
large round-sometimes flat/conical
flowering group 4   partial tip-bearing

 group 5

Another green Norfolk classic, but known for longer than Norfolk Beauty: it was first described by Forsyth in 1803 and introduced to the RHS in 1820. Although the cropping and keeping qualities do not match the Bramley, it is a striking apple in appearance and one of the finest cooking apples. The creamy flesh is sharp and full in flavour. The apples become greasy in storage, but last for two months, and can be enjoyed as a sharp spring dessert. The green hue turns a bright yellow when it is ready to pick in October. Note the lenticel spots which are rather scattered as a grey-green russet colour.

Because the shape is so regular they are ideal for showing and a tree in full fruit looks attractive in itself. Quickly into cropping and prolific later.

This is a famous old type and you are likely to find specimens in old orchards. A little russeting occurs around the fruit base. Look for very short stalks and well-rounded cells when cut open. Hogg (1884) noted that Sir Thomas Harr of Stowe Hall, Norfolk, procured it through his gardener from a tree, supposed to be the original, in an old orchard at Downham. He then passed it to the RHS. Taylor notes with relish: 'Cooks frothily and to a golden colour. It requires very little sugar'. The blossom is ornamental, but is susceptible to late frosts. The leaves are mid-green, bluntly serrated and downy.

GROUP 6
Stark's Earliest

dessert J F M A M J **J A** S O N D
medium-small   flat-round - round-conical
flowering group 1   freely spur-bearing

Now being sold as Scarlet Pimpernel. A smaller and earlier version of Gascoyne's Scarlet in looks, this was a chance cultivar found by Douglas Bonner at Orofino, Idaho, USA, in 1938 and introduced by the Stark Nurseries in 1944. Ripe at about the same time as Beauty of Bath, but better lasting, with good flavour and heavy cropping. Needs care in picking because it bruises easily (although this can be said of all apples).

Discovery (overleaf) has taken much of the market from this apple, and, having planted both, I can see why it has been edged out for keeping quality: the flavour fades more quickly. The blossom is pale pink and very like Discovery. Note, too, the creamy-yellow base hue and scarlet flush with numerous lenticel russet spots all over the surface. The stalk is medium length and surrounded by faint ribbing.

The skin is smooth and dry. It should be enjoyed fresh if possible and the flesh is white, aromatic, soft, fine-textured, juicy and sweet-sharp. The leaves are light green, serrated and flat rather than undulating, as in Lady Sudeley, for example. It has one of the earliest flowering times.

Gladstone

dessert J F M A M J **J A** S O N D
medium round-conical
flowering group 4   tip and spur bearing

 group 6

and it is one of the earliest of the summer dessert apples, to be picked and enjoyed straight from the tree. They do not keep more than a few days. The juice rapidly evaporates and the flesh goes soft almost at once. Old orchards may well have this variety because it was popular and widely grown. Hogg remarks on its attractive, strong aroma in summer, which fills the air around the tree. He notes that because it was ripe in the third week of July and was of such good flavour, with an appealing red colour, it was very popular in the fruit markets. Flushed dark red with stripes over green when ripe. Sometimes the apples are more streaky red if the light has not been enough to produce a deep red hue over the major surface of the fruit. The lenticel dots show up best on the green as red or purple dots. The skin is smooth, but becomes greasy. It has a bright pink blossom and the leaves are mid-green, oval, serrated and very downy on the underside.

Although it has been known from about 1780, it was first introduced to the trade by Jackson's Nursery, Kidderminster, Worcestershire, as 'Jackson's Seedling', then 'Mr Gladstone' after being awarded an RHS First Class Certificate in 1883. Now it is just known as 'Gladstone'.

A famous long-lived old type with a distinct raspberry taste. The original tree was still cropping well at over 100 years,

Discovery

dessert J F M A M J J **A S** O N D
medium - small   flat - round-flat
flowering group 3   tip and spur-bearing

group 6

A modern Essex cross of about 1949 produced this excellent and popular summer apple. Thought to be cultivated from Beauty of Bath and Worcester Pearmain, it was named in 1962 and introduced in 1963 by Matthew fruit trees, Thurston, Bury St Edmunds, Suffolk.

The mature tree crops well and is one I always recommend for a garden site as long as it does not get shaded. Fruit is slow to bear, but then very reliable and of all the summer apples, is one of the longest lasting early desserts in the fruit bowl. No early apples can be kept in *long* storage, but this probably comes the nearest to doing so.

It has an attractive pale blossom, symmetrical and flushed crimson over the pale green base colour. There are stripes in amongst the red (see photograph), but these largely disappear as the sun deepens the colour intensity of the fruit. Unlike some early types, the fruit does not drop before ripening.

Sweet, with creamy-white flesh and a pleasant juicy texture. The flavour makes the first summer tastings from the tree a real treat. Note the short stalk above russet cavity and yellow lenticel dots.

69

Laxton's Early Crimson

dessert J F M A M J J *A* S O N D
medium conical-long conical
flowering group 2 partial tip-bearing

 group 6

This deep-crowned apple was grown in 1908 at Bedford from a cross by the Laxton Brothers between Gladstone (p.68) and Worcester Pearmain (p.73). It shares the same elongated apex with Red Delicious (p.90) and Adam's Pearmain (p.118). The tree was introduced in 1931 and may be found in old orchards of this vintage. It is no longer grown commercially.

From my experience it has inherited the quality of Gladstone and should be enjoyed as picked because the fruit does not store. It has the sweet scent of its parents. (The Thomas Laxton family apples often seem to share a distinct flavour and are delicious when ripe. As they came to produce many apple varieties in Bedfordshire, their friends and neighbours in Hertfordshire, the Thomas Rivers family, cultivated more plum types, although both specialised in all sorts of fruit.)

The yellow-green base colour is flushed crimson and the lenticel spots show up as red against the pale green. Note the pronounced ribs at the tapering apex. It has pale pink blossom with thick green, narrow, serrated, leaves. They are very downy underside. It has a medium long, fairly slender stalk.

Duchess's Favourite

dessert J F M A M J J **A S** O N D
medium-small flat-round
flowering group 3 spur-bearing

Known from the late 1700s and early 1800s, at Addlestone in Surrey, it was acclaimed by the then Duchess of York – thus its name. (From the similar lenticel spots you might suspect that this was one of the uncertain parents of Discovery.)

Despite a rather thick skin and delicate flavour, this was a popular sweet apple with white flesh that sold well in London from the commercial Kent orchards. A garden variety now and attractive for summer shows. The blossom is pale, like Discovery, but the light green leaves are not so downy underneath. They are very symmetrical and have only a hint of ribbing. The lenticels are obvious as russet dots and there is also russeting round the rather short stalk.

A good variety for the West Country where it is most likely to be found due to its tolerance of wet and windy weather conditions. When the apple is cut open, the cell is found to be well rounded and the pips are numerous. The smooth skin can become greasy. The red hue is deep and bright crimson.

Devonshire Quarrenden

dessert J F M A M J J **A S** O N D
small flat-round
flowering group 2 spur-bearing

 group 6

First described in 1678 and again in 1690, this is a favourite Devonshire apple, possibly from the Carentan district in France. (Say Carentan with a heavy Devon accent.) It has a strong, aromatic, sweet flavour, both crisp and juicy.

Although the Worcester Pearmain is cited in many apple paternity cases, on this occasion we probably have one of the parents of the famous Worcester itself. Hogg was very enthusiastic about its success throughout Britain and in the most difficult of climatic conditions. Furthermore, it lasted to the end of September and he reported that the largest fruit to form were found in Herefordshire. With a green–yellow ground colour, the hue is distinctly Worcester purple-red and the lenticel spots around the stalk show up as purple russet patches. There is a green tinge to the flesh and the cell of opened specimens is rather pear-shaped.

The stalk is medium in length and rather thick. The shape of the apple is a little irregular, with angular ribs in some examples. The skin is smooth but becomes greasy if stored. The small, pale blossom is four days before Cox's Orange Pippin. The leaves are yellow-green, in part sharply, in others bluntly serrated. They are upward folding and very downy underneath.

Worcester Pearmain

dessert J F M A M J J A **S O** N D
medium conical-round-conical
flowering group 3   tip-bearing with some spurs

group 6

Raised (possibly from a Devonshire Quarrenden seedling) in Worcester in 1874, and given RHS First Class Certificate in 1875. An old favourite, especially eaten freshly picked. Bright red when allowed to mature, tapering and slightly ribbed. There is a distinct aroma and they are full of juicy flavour unless kept too long. Usually picked for sale too early. The flesh is white and sweet with fine texture. It has been our most popular early autumn dessert apple for over a hundred years. Skin smooth and greasy if stored. Light lenticel patches on the red flush which covers a pale green base. I have found the trees prone to scab on our London clay, but they are said to be resistant to mildew and hardy for growing in the north.

The trees sport attractive pale blossom and bright green, thin, broadly serrated leaves with downy undersides. Cropping is regular and heavy. A tree famous for taste and for being one of the parents of several other great apples, including Exeter Cross, Katy, Lord Lambourne, Merton Worcester, Michaelmas Red, Pearl, Tydeman's Early, William Crump and Winston.

Merton Knave
dessert J F M A M J J A **S** O N D
medium-small round
flowering group 3   partial tip-bearing

 group 6

Cultivated in 1948 from a cross between two Laxton types: Early Crimson and Epicure by M.B. Crane in London. In 1968 it was called Merton Ace, but quickly re-named in 1970 as Merton Knave. As with Tydeman's Early, there is a strawberry flavour, but it has a more delicate tang. Juicy, sweet and aromatic, the fruit crops regularly and the tree is hardy. The fruit can easily be mistaken for Worcester Pearmain or Tydeman's Early, but the bright red has an attractive shiny glow. Enjoy the pleasant flavour as soon as possible, because it will not last and the apples become very greasy in storage. Look for the yellow–green base colour, although the vivid red hue is fairly uniform. The lenticel dots are a guide because they are dark red or brown rather than pale as in similar bright red apples.

The fruit is generally symmetrical, ideal to show and has a very long stalk. It has creamy white flesh with a pink tinge which can be confused with Red Devil, a recent introduction. The blossom is pale pink and the dark green leaves are quite small, bluntly serrated, very upward folding and downy.

Merton Worcester

dessert J F M A M J J A **S O** N D
medium-small round-conical
flowering group 3 freely spur-bearing

group 6

Another great success by M.B. Crane at the John Innes Institute in London and named in 1948. (Gavin was also cultivated by the Institute, at Bayford, Hertfordshire, in 1956.) It received the RHS Merit Award in 1950, but its commercial exploitation trailed off when it was found to be prone to bitter pit disease. It is also on the small side for sale in the modern markets. Vigorous and quite hardy, the trees produce regular and heavy crops. The apples are sweet, strongly scented with hint of pear or strawberry in the aroma. Flesh is creamy, crisp texture and juicy. The problem with bitter pit is a concern, but it is upright in growth to make it suitable as a garden tree where space is limited.

Look for the pale yellow-tinged green base colour which yellows even more with ripening. Keeps a little longer than most of the early, bright red Worcester types, but becomes rather greasy in storage. There are little russet areas scattered across the smooth and initially dry skin and the lenticel dots are less conspicuous than in other reds, but show up well enough as pale brown with strong side lighting. They are generally very symmetrical in shape with a flattening to the apex where it also becomes faintly ribbed. Blossom is pale and leaves bright green, rather small, with faintly downy undersides.

Tydeman's Early
dessert J F M A M J J **A S** O N D
medium round-round-conical
flowering group 3 spur-bearing, but some tip-bearing

 group 6

First known from 1929 as Tydeman's Early Worcester from a cross H.M. Tydeman developed at East Malling Research Station in Kent between Worcester Pearmain and McIntosh. Introduced in 1945 and now successfully grown commercially in a number of countries.

You can see from its shape and colour that the Worcester and McIntosh looks are equally shared and in this case the qualities have survived well, too. It ripens ahead of Worcester (10 days earlier, according to Taylor) and seems to be less prone to disease on some types of soil. This is one to spare heavy pruning early on because an otherwise heavy cropper will produce less fruit in later years if the laterals (young side branches) are fiercely removed. Look for a long stalk, smooth skin becoming greasy in storage, slightly puckered apex basin and pips which narrow to a sharp point.

I particularly like the strawberry aroma and rich, full taste. The flesh is creamy, of good crisp texture and juicy. The skin is a pale green and yellows with maturity, but the deep crimson flush, almost purple in hue, covers most of the ripe apple. There is pale russet around the stalk and lenticels. The fruit is symmetrical, only occasionally lop-sided, and the blossom is the typical pale colour so many early apples seem to feature. There are bright grey-green leaves with downy undersides.

There is some commercial marketing still in this country and they are widely sold in Canada, USA and France as a popular early type.

Katy

dessert J F M A M J J A *SO* N D
medium conical
flowering group 3   freely spur-bearing

group 6

Cultivated 1947 in Sweden from a cross between James Grieve and Worcester Pearmain. Re-named from Katja and introduced in 1968, this will not, therefore, be that elusive red apple to be identified in a very old orchard. It has more vigour than Worcester Pearmain and is a very attractive fruit that pollinates well with other varieties in the vicinity. Crops heavily and benefits from thinning to increase the fruit size. It has been a commercial success and is hardy for growth in the north. Although the skin is thick and the flavour is delicate rather than strong, it is, however, a very refreshing apple inheriting the firmness of its Worcester ancestor and the acidity of James Grieve. It will not last as the flesh goes soft soon after being picked.

Like its James Grieve parent, the greenish-yellow skin hue becomes a custard yellow as it ripens. Bright crimson covers most of the fruit and the lenticels do not show very clearly when compared with Discovery. We grow both types near each other.

Look for a yellow-ochre russeting around the stalk which is usually set at a slight angle. Smooth, dry skin, greasy if stored. The shape is symmetrical, but occasionally slightly uneven and faintly ribbed. The blossom makes an ornamental pink and the leaves are mid-green.

Herring's Pippin
dual J F M A M J J A **S O N** D
large round-conical
flowering group 4   freely spur-bearing

 group 6

Attributed to W.A. Herring of Lincoln, October 1908, when he exhibited them at the RHS show of that year. Sold by the J.R. Pearson Nursery of Lowdham, Nottingham, from 1917. Received the RHS Award of Merit in 1920.

A fairly vigorous, upright-spreading tree which crops well, but needs to be thinned to retain size in years of very heavy production. There are mixed views on its flavour, but it is generally spicy with a hint of aniseed reminiscent of a ripe Ellison's Orange. They are very hardy and make good cooking apples, too. Look for a large size and bright red hue over a pale base colour of greenish-yellow. The flush covers most of the fruit and there are broken red stripes within the colour. The lenticel dots show up as white specks. The skin is very smooth and becomes greasy in storage. The flesh is creamy white, rather soft, with a coarse texture. The pips are quite large and rather flat. The stalk is short and stout.

The blossom is large and bright pink. The leaves are medium to large, mid-green, narrow, sometimes upward folding and rather undulating to the touch. Note the blunt serrations and downy underside. Fairly downy.

McIntosh Red

dessert J F M A M J J A **S O N D**
medium-*large* round-flat-round
flowering group 2   very freely spur-bearing

group 6

First reported as a chance seedling in 1796 near Dundela, Dundas County, Ontario, Canada, by John McIntosh and later propagated by Allan McIntosh in 1870. Although it is the parent of several outstanding types here and is very successful commercially in Canada and USA, in Britain it is liable to canker. The apples are attractive on the tree, with a bright purple red hue on a lemon green base; the lenticel spots show up as light pink spots and there are stripes within the red flushed area. In the cell the seeds are rather large in proportion to the rest of the apple which can be a little irregular and lop-sided. The stalk is short and fairly slender. The aromatic skin is smooth and dry.

Note that the white flesh is tinged pink when cut or bitten and the flavour tends towards a mixture of strawberry and elderflower. They are very juicy and there is a slightly soft, fine texture. The blossom is pale pink and the leaves light yellow-green. They have a slight upward fold, are medium thick with blunt serrations and are very downy underneath.

Gascoyne's Scarlet

dual **J** F M A M J J A **S O N D**
medium-large   round-oblong
flowering group 5   partial tip-bearing

 group 6

Most authors fail to point out the great advantage of this tree: it is ideal on a pure chalk soil. Cultivated not, as I once thought, from one of the Gascoyne Cecil estates, but, Bunyard, 1920, explains: 'by Mr Gascoyne of Sittingbourne, Kent, and introduced in 1871 by the firm of Geo. Bunyard.' Awarded RHS First Class Certificate in 1887. I always try to have Gascoyne's Scarlet on show at our Apple Days because it is grown at our local Shenley Orchard and is very attractive. Eaten from the tree it is refreshing in a slightly sharp way and cooks well. Bultitude says it is sweet, with little flavour, but that sounds like a late tasting: a dual apple tends to lose flavour as the acidity disappears.

Look for the bright pale green base colour which yellows and the third to three quarters of scarlet hue. Lenticel dots show up well on both colours: green or russet. Slightly greasy in storage. Medium stalk. Regular shape; flesh tinged faint green, fine texture and juicy. Good show and garden variety.

Norfolk Royal

dessert J F M A M J J A **S O N D**
medium-large conical-long-conical
flowering group 5 partial tip-bearing

group 6

Once a familiar East Anglian type and popular for shows, but now quite scarce. Cultivated by Wright's Nursery, North Walsham in Norfolk in 1908, but not named until 1930. A type likely to turn up in old orchards in East Anglia, it is striking when ripening. The vigorous, upright trees crop very well and the flavour is pleasant, crisp and very juicy. If well thinned the fruit will be a good size and Taylor described the apples as looking as if they had been 'varnished'. He also considered that they kept well until February, which is a great bonus for such an early sweet apple, and very unusual. December is probably about the usual length of keeping time, without special chilling facilities.

Look for a bright scarlet hue, about pillar box red, pale yellow on the shaded parts, short broken red stripes and small white lenticel dots. The shape is very symmetrical with lop-sided variations and there are generally about five crowns at the apex. The trees have late, pale pink blossom and medium sized, upward folding mid to yellow–green leaves, quite downy underneath. There is blunt serration to the leaf edges rather than a sharp ribbing effect. The shiny skin is slightly greasy and the white flesh soon stains pink when the apple is cut open.

Mother

dessert J F M A M J J A **S O** N D
medium long-conical
flowering group 5   freely spur-bearing

 group 6

Introduced from America by Thomas Rivers about 150 years ago from a tree recorded in 1844. Distinguished by its colour and shape, the fruit is also very juicy, sweet and well scented. Flesh is quite soft.

An excellent October dessert variety for looks and taste. The trees are fairly upright , which make it a good garden variety, although the cropping is rather irregular. Recommended as a good West Country fruit, it will often ripen to the deep purple red of the Worcester. Generally, a yellow-green base colour is retained over part of the very oval fruit and the red appears as a mottled red hue.

Look for ribbing and flattening at the apex, with a short and rather slender stalk. There are numerous, plump pips in a round cell and the lenticel dots appear as very fine russet specks. The blossom is a fairly strong pink which is more typical of the mid season sweet apples. The leaves are grey-green with a little down underneath. Taylor notes that the waxy bloom on the fruit when growing disappears on keeping.

Emperor Alexander

dessert J F M A M J J A **S O** N D
very large round-conical-conical
flowering group 3 partial tip-bearer

group 6

Hogg described this apple, also known as Alexander, as 'handsome and most esteemed by exhibitors'. Named by the growers round the Baltic who used to send the fruit to the Czar Alexander I at the Russian Court as a compliment. Ukraine was probably the origin of the apple which has existed at least since the 1700s. Introduced in London in 1805 by James Lee.

Can be enjoyed as an aromatic, juicy, brisk dessert. The white flesh with greenish-lemon tinge cooks to a pale yellow pulp. The flavour is still sweet, but rather bland. The skin, which is smooth and dry, has a pale grass-green tinge with attractive bright red flush. There are broken red stripes and splashes of the same hue. The lenticels spots are pale brown and become more frequent and paler towards the apex. The stalk is fairly stout. The apples can become greasy in storage.

The blossom is pale pink and the leaves are medium to large, broadly serrated and quite thick. The mid-green, downy leaves have an undulating surface and tend to fold upwards slightly.

Spartan

dessert **J F** M A M J J A S **O N D**
medium round-conical
flowering group 3 spur-bearing

 group 6

Familiar maroon eating apple grown in Canada and Britain following the cross at the Dominion Experiment Station, Summerland, British Columbia, Canada between a McIntosh and Yellow Newtown Pippin by R. C. Palmer, 1926. Introduced in 1936 and found to be heavy cropping and best grown on M9 and M26 rootstocks. (Remember that M26 does not like heavy clay soils.) Prone to canker, but a fairly vigorous and upright growing tree which also suits gardens, including in the west and north. The shiny, deep purple red fruit has a bloom before you polish it up and is a characteristic to look for. The ground colour is pale whitish green which yellows and the skin is tough, smooth and dry. There is a distinct strawberry aroma and a melon flavour, according to taste.

It usually has five crowns to distinct ribs and may be lop-sided from growth competition. So prolific that the fruits can crowd and the tree benefits from thinning to maintain size. The stalk is medium in length and width, extending just above the fruit. Lenticel dots show up well as scattered white specks. It has pale blossom and medium light green leaves, very downy underneath. The fruit keeps well from an early October picking, although gradually loses juiciness in storage.

Gala

dessert **J** F M A M J J A S **O N D**
medium oblong-conical
flowering group 4 freely spur-bearing

group 6

We are probably as familiar with the sport of this apple, Royal Gala, which is imported and sold in large quantities due to its good texture. J.H. Kidd cultivated this cross in 1934 between Kidd's Orange Red and Golden Delicious at Greytown, Wairarapa, in New Zealand. It was named in 1965 and, although it is prone to scab, the fairly vigorous, upright and open trees do well, even in the north.

Not only is it a commercial success, therefore, but it is ideal for gardens and shows, too. It is worth thinning the heavy crops, which hang attractively, to increase their size and reduce its biennial tendency. Look for the intensity of the orange–red which is speckled with more red over a pale green base that turns golden yellow as it ripens. The stalk varies somewhat in length, but is usually long and thin. There are some small patches of russet and the lenticels spots show up as pale brown dots. The skin is smooth, but becomes a little greasy in storage, which can extend to January. The aromatic flesh is creamy, very sweet and crisp. It owes much of its fine taste to the Cox's Orange Pippin ancestry on the Kidd's Orange Red side. The pips are fairly large for the apple and plump in shape. The blossom is very pale and the thin leaves are dark–green, narrow, upward folding and serrated. Their undersides are pale green, but not very downy.

Jonathan
dessert J F M A M J J A S **O N D**
small-medium round-oblong
flowering group 3   freely spur-bearing

 group 6

Described from 1826 (and alternatively spelt Jonathon), the origin is thought to be a cross from Esopus Spitzenberg on a farm owned by Philip Rick, Woodstock, New York, USA. It was named after Jonathan Hasbrouk who reported the tree.

With heavy, regular cropping and a refreshing flavour, it is a commercial success and well known in many countries. There is resistance to scab, but the trees are susceptible to apple mildew, *Podosphaera leucotricha*. (I have found the sealed plastic tree protectors create many such problems with apples and wire tree tubes are much better for air circulation.) Similar in shape and size to Kent, they tend to be rather smaller and more distinctly five crown ribbed. Flattened sides with many large pips. Note smaller stalk compared with Kent, p.99.

White flesh, slightly green tinged, sweet-sharp, juicy, fine texture and almost a pear-drop aroma. The thick skin shines and is smooth and dry. There is a pale green base hue with bright crimson flush over most of the apple. Note the red stripes, some russet patches and faint lenticel dots. The blossom is high pink and the leaves deep cut in places on their serrated edges. They are very downy underneath.

Idared

dual **J F M A** M J J A S **O N D**
medium - large flat-round
flowering group 2 very freely spur-bearing

group 6

Not 'I dared', but named 'Ida-red', referring to its cultivation by Leif Verner at Idaho Agricultural Experimental Station, USA, as a cross between Jonathan (opposite) and Wagener (p.55). Introduced in 1942 after trials commenced in 1935. Commercial success has followed because of its very long keeping and dual purpose features, although it can have a rather chewy, weak, if crisp, flavour. Resists scab, is hardy and crops well.

The shiny, smooth, dry skin has a pale green ground colour which yellows in storage. The apples have a purple red hue and stripes which show on the more shaded side of the fruit. Ribbing shows as a rather lumpy surface and the gloss is a feature when you polish the fruit.

Note how the stalk is slender and the lenticel dots are rather indistinct as pale flecks. Russet free except where there has been minor marking during the growing season. The blossom is a fairly strong pink; the light green leaves, serrated, fold upwards generally and are downy underneath. Fresh and juicy, it also cooks with a good flavour.

The longest keeping apple I know: Harold Bland stored some for eighteen months.

Mère de Ménage
cooking **J F** M A M J J A **S** O N **D**
large flat-round
flowering group 3 partial tip-bearing

group 6

Known from the late 18th century, it is distinct from the French variety of the same name. I was struck by its irregular shape, size and colour when I first saw a basket display of them at Brogdale. They are well flavoured, but during cooking the flesh loses its sparkle. The trees, ideal in a garden, grow very upright and they crop well. They show well and, if kept stored, have a long season. The success of Bramley's Seedling rather eclipsed this 'Valuable and very beautiful culinary apple of first rate quality' in Hogg's words from 1884. It has a sharp, rather coarse, dry texture with pale green base colour.

Look for the irregular shape, frequently lop–sided, deep red flush, stripes and speckles. The stalk is quite short and stout on very large fruit. Skin smooth and dry with some pale russeting round the stalk. There are sometimes as much as seven crowns at the apex, although five is more usual. It has obvious, white lenticel spots. The blossom is pale and the dark green leaves are large, serrated, with downy undersides.

John Standish

dessert **J F** M A M J J A S **O** N **D**
medium round-round-conical
flowering group 3 spur-bearing

group 6

This apple's colour resembles that of Gascoyne's Scarlet, (p.80), but its season is later and the fruit is smaller and rounder. It is said to have been grown by John Standish in Ascot, Berkshire, about 1873. It received the RHS Award of Merit in 1922. Although it is reliable and keeps well, some find the flavour weak, even absent, whilst others, including me, say it is 'fruity'. The tree is both hardy and vigorous, with the apples keeping well into the next year.

The shiny skin becomes rather greasy in storage. Look for the pale yellow-green base colour which becomes flushed with a bright crimson red. The lenticel dots show up very clearly as light grey or yellow speckling, also like the dots on Gascoyne's Scarlet. Apart from an occasional single rib, the shape is regular, only slightly lop-sided.

The skin is chewy, the flesh is white, firm, fine-textured and juicy. There is a slight aroma. The stalk is medium in length and swells where it joins with the spur. The blossom is an attractive pink and the leaves are dark to mid-green, serrated and downy underneath.

Red Delicious

dessert **J F** M A M J J A S **O** N **D**
medium-large oblong-oblong-conical
flowering group 3 spur-bearing

 group 6

Best in sunny, light climates, this is the most grown apple in the world now – featured in many variations or sports from the original Delicious, discovered about 1880 in Iowa, USA. It was growing as a shoot from a rootstock and as I am one who all too often has allowed such faults in apple cultivation, it is good to know what a success can come by chance. It is a pity that all the best of these Delicious sports so far become rather woody in our climate, but cropping is good and the trees are vigorous. If you have a very warm, light site, this would be worth trying even if very dwarfed in a pot. It has pale lenticel spots all over the deep, attractive red hue. Look for a long, stout stalk, very obvious ribbing and a frequent lop-sided appearance. The striking shiny purple red comes when you rub the bloom off and is on a base of yellow-green. The skin is tough, smooth and dry.

It has creamy flesh with a green tinge, is fine textured, highly aromatic, juicy and very sweet. It is not surprising that this apple is so widely grown and exported to us. The blossom is pale. The leaves are a striking dark green, bluntly serrated. They fold upwards slightly and are fairly downy underneath.

William Crump

dessert **J F** M A M J J A S **O** N **D**
medium-large round-conical
flowering group 5   spur-bearing

group 6

Two famous apples were crossed by William Crump at Madresfield Court Gardens, Malvern, Worcestershire, to create this apple: Worcester Pearmain and Cox's Orange Pippin. It was exhibited on 22nd December 1908 and awarded an RHS First Class Certificate a year later. Taylor noted the very thin russet on the unexposed skin and the excellent fruit taste which is pineapple-like. The late flowering time and long keeping are valuable in a winter dessert, particularly in areas that are susceptible to frosts. A vigorous tree, but it does not crop heavily. The fruit has one of the most intense, rich flavours of all eaters. The flesh is creamy, very aromatic, of firm texture, juicy and sweet. It has that good balance between the sugars and sharpness which all the great apples possess.

Look for a pale green fruit, yellowing to a deep custard base hue, purple flush, with indistinct stripes and pale russet lenticel dots. The shape flattens noticeably at each end. Smooth, shiny skin, becoming greasy in storage. It has a pale blossom and mid-green leaves which are upward folding and very downy.

GROUP 7
Laxton's Epicure
dessert J F M A M J **A S** O N D
medium flat-round-round-conical
flowering group 3 spur-bearing

It is now listed just as Epicure, but it is one of the Laxton Brothers' very best crosses, using Cox's Orange Pippin and Wealthy, in 1909, and introduced in 1929. It received the RHS Award of Merit in 1931.

This is the first of the reinette group of apples, which have some russet, but not enough for them to be classified with the russets.

Although this excellent sweet August apple has a long stout stalk and broken red lines, its pale green base hue and broken red stripes can flush full crimson to confuse. Look for inconspicuous lenticel dots except on red fruit where they show up as light brown russet flecking. The trees are upright and fairly vigorous with a tendency to over-crop and produce, biennially, large numbers of small apples. I find them delicious when freshly picked and the flavour is delicately aromatic, even pear-like. This is lost even in short storage. The skin is smooth and dry. The flesh is creamy-white and juicy with a tang of Cox. It has a bright pink, ornamental blossom and pollinates well with Bramley. It is also a useful tree in colder districts where they show good frost resistance. The leaves are thick, leathery, dark green, serrated to broadly-serrated and have little down on the underside.

Merton Beauty

dessert J F M A M J J A **S O** N D
medium-small flat-round
flowering group 5 freely spur-bearing

group 7

A 1933 cross by M.B. Crane with Ellison's Orange (which is itself already the result of a Cox-cross) and Cox's Orange Pippin, at the John Innes Institute, London. Promoted from 1962, it retains the Ellison's hint of aniseed flavour and has been described as 'truly delicious, if idiosyncratic'. (I made the mistake of planting our garden tree in too much shade and we have had few to enjoy so far). It crops well from an upright tree.

The flesh is creamy-white, of firm texture and the juicy taste is distinctive. It is sweet, melting and aromatic. Note that the pips are large for the size of the fruit. It has the Cox/Ellison-look in size and shape, but is bright dark red on a pale yellow-green base colour. There are mottled red stripes and the lenticel dots are indistinct. They are flecked by russet patches, with a fairly long, stout stalk. Late flowering helps in frost pockets. The apples are a regular, even shape with little or no ribbing. The blossom is pale pink and the leaves are mid-green, thick and leathery, with regular serrations along the leaf edge and only a little down underneath.

93

Merton Charm

dessert J F M A M J J A **SO** N D
medium-small round-round-conical
flowering group 2 freely spur-bearing

 group 7

The fourth of M.B. Crane's crosses selected as outstanding in this book (see Merton Beauty, previous page, of a more orange hue, but early to crop like the first two, pp.74,75). Cultivated in 1933 from a cross between Ellison's Orange and Cox's Orange Pippin. Because Ellison's also has Cox parentage, this is quite a mixture, but the constant mixing and re-mixing has been part of the remarkable, yet little recognised story of dedicated fruit development over the centuries. The tree is more spreading than the other sweet Merton types, but it crops very well and regularly. The flavour actually increases as these juicy apples age. They have a strong aroma and delicate texture. If you have space for a spreading tree in the garden, it is an excellent choice and the small fruit make ideal snacks for children. They are really refreshing picked and eaten from the tree in September, but do last another month if kept cool.

Note the pale green base which is only partly dull red, long thin leaves, broadly serrated and rather darker blossom than similar small red sweet apples. There are some pale brown lenticel spots which show up on the green areas of the smooth, dry skin. The flesh is creamy white with a fine texture.

Ellison's Orange
dessert J F M A M J A **S O** N D
medium round-slightly conical
flowering group 4 spur-bearing

group 7

Cultivated by Rev C.C. Ellison at Bracebridge, Lincolnshire, and Mr Wipf, the gardener at Hartsholme Hall in 1904 by crossing Cox's Orange Pippin with Calville Blanc. It gained an RHS First Class Certificate in 1917. It is of excellent flavour and, although it is said to be very susceptible to canker, our over-grown 70-year-old cordons at Tewin are still able to produce good crops even where canker is now endemic. At first sight they are easily confused with one of the parents, the Cox, but the aniseed flavour, which is said to be stronger the more brightly coloured the fruit, is the quickest guide. Also look for a variable stalk length and width whereas the Cox tends to be a medium length. The base colour is light green-yellow which deepens in yellow hue as it ripens. They are flushed in variable degrees with orange-red and broken stripes.

The skin is smooth and greasy - very greasy after storage. The flesh is cream, juicy, crisp, aromatic with the intense flavour described above. There is a delicate pink blossom and light green leaves, serrated with blunt edges and slightly upward folding; they are not very downy underneath.

Laxton's Fortune

dessert J F M A M J J A *S O* N D
medium round-slightly conical
flowering group 3 fairly freely spur-bearing

 group 7

Listed as Fortune now, but one of the best cross pollinations by the Laxton Brothers in Bedford, 1904, using Wealthy and Cox's Orange Pippin. RHS First Class Certificate in 1948. It is no longer commercially grown because it is best picked ripe and will go soft if stored from early harvest. Pick your own is ideal or garden consumption direct from the tree. It is very vigorous, upright spreading and of excellent flavour 'to rival Worcester' in Taylor's view. It has creamy flesh, sweet, juicy and aromatic as long as ripe: woody and dull if picked too early. It suits some areas (the North and West) more than others, but is quite hardy. Our trees cropped well for about 60 years in the South East, but for unknown reasons they do less well in certain southern localities.

Look for a similar yellowing and colouring as James Grieve when ripe, but it has a green base hue and red stripe broken on a crimson flush until then. There are areas of russet on the dry, smooth skin. The stalk length and thickness is also similar. Lenticel spots are inconspicuous, tiny grey russet specks. The blossom is not such an intense pink as James Grieve, but well coloured and the leaves are mid-green. They are serrated in blunt points and noticeably oval in shape, not very downy underneath.

Fiesta (Red Pippin)

dessert **J** F M A M J J A **S O** N **D**
medium-small round-flat-round
flowering group 3 spur-bearing

group 7

A fairly recent cross between Cox's Orange Pippin and Idared at East Malling, Kent. It gained a Preliminary Commendation by the RHS in 1987. The tree is hardy and part self-fertile. It is a late dessert of excellent flavour, picked early, but enjoyed into the new year. At 'Elbourn Apples', Meldreth near Royston, Hertfordshire, it is called 'Red Pippin', which is really what it is, especially in looks and taste. With heavy cropping on moderately vigorous, upright spreading trees, and the rich Cox flavour, this is a very successful mixture of types and the bright red may cause confusion in future orchards. The long stalk, which is often set at an angle, is a guide and the shape is very Cox-like. A refreshing small to medium sized apple, ideal for children.

Look for some russet on the smooth skin round the stalk cavity, the orange base colour as it ripens, and a large crimson flush with purple stripes that cover most of the apple. The lenticel dots do not show very well, but appear as pale pink-white specks.

The flesh is creamy, like a Cox, and aromatic with a juicy sweet-sharp tang. The blossom is pale pink and the leaves are dark green to yellow-green. They are serrated and downy underneath.

Lord Lambourne

dessert J F M A M J J A *SO* N D
medium round - slightly conical
flowering group 2 produces spurs freely

 group 7

Another successful cross by the Laxton Brothers of Bedford. Grown in 1907 from James Grieve and Worcester Pearmain. Tactfully named after a President of the RHS and awarded their Bunyard Cup and Award of Merit when introduced in 1923. An excellent cropper of high quality, even-sized fruit which are now largely disease-free after early problems. It has a refreshing taste of strawberry. The flesh is white, tinged with cream, sweet-sharp, juicy and aromatic. Look for very obvious pale grey or russet lenticel spots across the fruit, which is pale green covered by a bright red flush and broken red stripes. They do not keep beyond mid-November and becomes very greasy if stored.

The rather broad pips are large and numerous. There is a slender, medium length stalk. The shape of the apple is regular with a hint of ribs and corrugated with five crown bumps. It has an ornamental, strong pink blossom. The light green leaves are medium in size, broad, bluntly serrated and fairly thick. They are also flat and upward folding. The undersides are slightly downy.

Kent

dessert **J F** M A M J J A S **O N D**
medium round-conical-conical
flowering group 3   freely spur-bearing

group 7

Known as Malling Kent when named in 1974, this is one of the great Malling cultivars developed by H.M. Tydeman at the East Malling Research Station in Kent during 1947. Not the easiest propagation year I would have thought as far as weather was concerned and the tree certainly does better in sunny years. Keeps well for a dessert apple and harvests around the National Apple Day 21 October.

The flavour is juicy and pleasant and the trees crop well. The red hue is very like Mère de Ménage, but the size is smaller and shape very regular in comparison. A neatly rounded and conical apple, well covered in colour on a pale green base with distinct ribs at the apex. The lenticel spots show up well as light russet spots on the red or as grey-brown on the green which yellows in storage.

The skin is tough, smooth and dry. The flesh is aromatic, cream coloured and has a firm texture. The brightly coloured blossom is well veined and the leaves are mid to grey-green. They are oval, unusually serrated every second gap, or bluntly serrated, with little down underneath.

Autumn Pearmain

dessert J F M A M J J A *S O N* D
medium conical
flowering group 4   partial tip-bearing

 group 7

One of the oldest desserts named by Hogg who gives 1629 for its first description and Bultitude thinks the late 1500s. Identical to the Herefordshire Pearmain, it has also been called Royal Pearmain and Summer Pearmain at different times. It crops heavily from upright spreading trees. Crawford describes the flesh as cream coloured, dry, firm, and nutty with quite a rich flavour. Look for a base colour of dull green which yellows as the fruit ripens. There is a flush of orange-red which intensifies. Broken stripes of bright red are overlaid by a netting of fine russet. The skin is, however, quite smooth and only becomes a little greasy in storage. Lenticel dots show up as light spots. Generally the fruit are rather lop-sided and flattened at the base. The stalk is medium length and stout. It is often set at an angle. The pips are plump.

There are faint ribs and five crowns slightly show at the apex. The blossom is bright pink and the leaves mid to dark green, slightly upward folding, serrated, fairly thick and undulating with a downy underside.

Cornish Aromatic

dessert **J F M** A M J J A S **O N D**
medium round-conical-oblong-conical
flowering group 4 freely spur-bearing

group 7

As with Cornish Gilliflower, this tree was found growing in Cornwall - by Sir Christopher Hawkins, who brought apples to show at the RHS in London in 1813. It is thought to have been known for centuries before this and is rather enigmatic: the flavour is of the highest aromatic quality some years, but in other years is chewy and bland. There is no actual aroma when cut. It crops well from a vigorous tree with upright spread and is ideal for the garden.

The apples are attractive enough to show and will store to the following spring. Note the five-crowned ribs at the apex and the pale green base colour which turns golden yellow as it ripens. There is a deep red flush and indistinct, broken red stripes. The lenticel spots are very obvious as a pale russet and give the skin a dry and slightly rough feel. The fruit is distinctly ribbed and conical, with a white flesh, tinged green. It is sweet-sharp, firm, dry and nutty at best.

The stalk is medium length and stout. The cell area of the core is as large as in Cornish Gilliflower and useful for reference. The blossom is pale pink and the leaves are mid-green, bluntly serrated and upward-folding. They are quite thick and undulating with a fair amount of down underneath.

Sunset

dessert J F M A M J J A **S O N D**
medium flat-round-round-conical
flowering group 3 freely spur-bearing

 group 7

Cultivated as an open-pollinated Cox's Orange Pippin seedling by G.C. Addy at Ightham, Kent, in 1918, it eventually received the RHS Award of Merit in 1960. It is best grown in a garden where a Cox has been found to dislike the soil and be subject to canker. It is a little too small for modern commercial success. Hardy and tolerant of wet areas, it is a heavy cropper from upward spreading, rather compact trees. Thinning helps to increase the crop size. The flavour is like an early Cox with good aroma and it is juicy, intense and crisp. It does best in dry areas with cool summers. They have the yellow and orange-red of Cox and Ellison's Orange, but with more russeting and lack the taste of aniseed you have with Ellison's. There are fewer red stripes than either. The shape is a good guide and they are like a flatter version of Cox. There is a textured feel to the dry skin.

The stalk is fairly long and stout, sometimes bumpy. The pips look large, as do Cox's. The blossom is pale pink, like both Cox and Ellison's. The leaves are medium to small, mid-green and rather oval in shape. They are bluntly and more broadly serrated than Cox and a little lighter in colour, slightly folding upwards. There is the same downy underside to the leaves as you find in the Cox.

Allington Pippin

dual, cider J F M A M J J A **S O N D**
medium-large conical
flowering group 3 spur-bearing

group 7

Taylor explains how Thomas Laxton's Lincolnshire cultivar was at first Brown's South Lincoln Beauty when shown by the Stamford nursery in 1889, but was exhibited again in 1894 when it received the RHS First Class Certificate. It was marketed under the new name by the Bunyard nursery. Taylor also notes that it was 'too sharp for the modern tastes, although the tree has many excellent features'. He does, however, praise its sweet cooking qualities and it is also a good cider apple. The flavour is richly aromatic and crunchy. The apples can be taken to be Laxton's Superb (p.115) because they share a rather dull colour, although the reds are a different hue. Look for a very pale green apple, ripening to lemon-yellow and a brownish-red flush. There are a few broken red stripes and the lenticels show up as light russet. There is more russet speckling on Laxton's Superb. Best as a dessert in December.

The flesh is creamy, fine textured, juicy and sharp. The smooth and dry skin is subject to 'Allington Spot' where the lenticels break down as brown speckles. Usually of fairly regular shape, they are occasionally lop-sided and there are faint traces of ribs at the apex. The blossom is pale pink and the leaves are light green, bluntly serrated and medium-thick. The undersides are fairly downy.

Holstein

dessert J F M A M J J A **S O N D**
medium large oblong-conical-round conical
flowering group 3 freely spur-bearing triploid

 group 7

An open-pollinated Cox's Orange Pippin was cultivated (or found) at Holstein in Germany by a Mr Vahldik, a teacher, in about 1918. It is like a very large Cox in colour and shape with similar highly aromatic flavour. It is triploid and needs two other apple trees in flower for pollination. The trees are vigorous and wide-spreading, but cropping is moderate. The fruit has a superb flavour from firm, juicy, sweet and creamy flesh. It has a coarser texture, but a stronger taste, than Cox. Look for the greenish-yellow base colour which ripens to a golden colour. This is flushed orange-red with broken crimson stripes and the lenticel spots are rather indistinct pale dots. (Sanders shows the strong yellow and striped hue and Bultitude illustrates a very red group.)

The stalk is short and stout and the pips look large and plump, sometimes rather withered-looking. They are sometimes lop-sided and flat at the base. The fruit becomes slightly greasy when kept. The blossom is bright pink and the leaves are large, blue-green and serrated. The leaf margins may curve upwards and the undersides are very downy. There are several other colour sports.

Lady Henniker
dual, cider J F M A M J J A **S O N D**
large oblong
flowering group 5 freely spur-bearing

group 7

Another slow to bear favourite I have planted many times, this distinctly angular Suffolk apple turns to a wonderful custard yellow with pink blush when fully ripe. Cultivated by John Perkins who was Lord Henniker's gardener, from a pip he found in cider must at Thornham Hall, Eye, about 1845. Introduced in 1873 and received the RHS First Class Certificate that year.

This apple has been compared to a large Ribston Pippin, but is oblong and often lop-sided in shape. It is strongly ribbed and one is often larger than the rest, creating rather flat-sides. It is five crowned at the apex. The stalk is short to medium and stout. The base colour is bright green before the golden yellow develops and the sun turns exposed sides to an orange-red flush. There are broken red speckles with hidden grey lenticel spots.

The flesh is creamy white, tinged with green and yellow under the skin. It has a brisk taste, cooking well with good flavour. They should be harvested promptly because the fruit tends to drop as it ripens. The blossom is ornamental and the leaves are mid-green, large, broad, serrated and downy.

Orleans Reinette

dessert **J F** M A M J J A S **O N D**
medium large flat-round
flowering group 4 spur-bearing

 group 7

Both Bunyard and Taylor point out that it can be confused with a Blenheim Orange with heavy russet markings, but that it is sweeter and richer in flavour: there is an orange tang followed by a pleasant walnut taste. In 1776, Knoop, the Dutch botanist, described the apple, but where it came from is not certain. It is probably French and received the RHS Award of Merit first as Winter Ribston in 1914 and then as Orleans Reinette in 1921.

The trees are vigorous and upward spreading, bear young and crop well, but beware the fruit drop as they ripen. It is possible to cook or liquidise these early windfalls. The creamy-white flesh is firm, sweet, aromatic and quite juicy. One of the best of all dessert apples. Although some large examples look like Blenheim Orange, check for dull green in the base colour (which turns golden), a faint flush of orange-red and indistinct, broken red stripes. On the skin there is a mottled texture of russet with large lenticel dots.

The apples are flattened top and tail with some traces of ribs. There is a short to medium, stout stalk. The blossom is pale pink and the leaves are large, oval, sharply serrated and dark green. They are not very downy underneath.

Blenheim Orange

dual **J** F M A M J J A S **O N D**
large flat-round
flowering group 3 spurs, but tendency to tip-bearing
triploid

group 7

It was found at the Woodstock near Blenheim in Oxfordshire by a Mr Kempster around 1740. It became available from 1818 and received the RHS Banksian Medal in 1822. I have planted a number of these trees and they are slow to crop, but I have never forgotten the first time I enjoyed the rare, nutty and aromatic flavour of the apple. The taste has been described as 'addictive' by some. In fact, the name needed the permission of the Duke of Marlborough since it was growing next to the wall at Blenheim. It was so sought for propagation that this was readily given. It is likely to be in many old orchards and gardens. The distinctive taste is ideal served with cheese. There is a speckling of russet over the pale green-yellow base colour, flushed with a dull orange-red.

The short and stout stalk turns to the side to peer over the cavity and the skin is smooth and dry. Note its rounded ribs. The flesh is creamy, sweet and crisp. They cook well. They are another triploid that crops heavily, although they can become biennial. The blossom is bright pink and makes an ornamental tree. The leaves are quite large, broad, oval, dark green, sharply serrated and downy.

Margil

dessert **J F** M A M J J A S **O N D**
small round-conical
flowering group 2 very freely spur-bearing

group 7

Taylor considered that although this apple was 'not handsome, it really is an excellent dessert'. It needs a sunny ripening time to do well here and this may be explained by its origin from a lighter district of Europe in 1750. The first tree described was in Sir William Temple's garden at Sheen in Surrey. They are ideal garden apples due to their weak growth which can be further restricted by dwarf rootstocks; use in a sunny and sheltered corner. Frosts can catch the early flowering, but with good warning, it is easy to protect a small tree. The taste has been compared with Ribston Pippin and the flesh is a deep cream colour, richly aromatic, sweet, juicy and crisp. Sunshine at the right time will intensify the flavour.

Look for a slightly lop-sided shape with angular, flat sides. They crop well and bunch attractively. Some of the fruits are five crowned from irregular ribs. The base colour is pale green-yellow, becoming golden, and there is a bright orange red flush. The red stripes are broad and there are russet patches. Lenticels show as pale dots. It has bright pink blossom, with grey-green, very downy leaves.

King of the Pippins

dessert, cider J F M A M J J A S **O N D**
medium oblong-conical
flowering group 5 freely spur-bearing

group 7

Like the baffling range of very similar-looking pippins, the origin of this apple is also confusing. Mr Kirke of Brompton, London, named it early in the 19th century, but it is thought to have been Golden Winter Pearmain, re-named. To make the origins even more uncertain, it seems to be identical with Reine des Reinettes (one of a group of high quality, late keeping French apples, often tinged with russet, called reinettes) of France. Not so popular in the last century as it had been, this apple is of excellent flavour with a slight underlying bitter tang. This gives it a very useful option as both as a cider apple and even a cooker, too. You may find it in old cider orchards, especially in the Midlands. The trees are vigorous, hardy and upright, suitable for the west country. Note the green-yellow to golden yellow, flushed brownish orange-red and short broken red stripes. The patches of scattered russet and spots round the lenticels show fairly well.

They are quite regular in shape, lop-sided at times, with rounded ribs. They grow well in large flower pots, too. The flesh is creamy white, firm, juicy with a brisk nutty, aromatic flavour. There is a medium length stalk and strong pink blossom. The leaves are blue-green, medium to small, serrated and flat. They are downy underneath.

group 7

One of the best of J.H. Kidd's New Zealand experiments in crossing the finest of English and American apples. It was raised in 1924 from Cox's Orange Pippin and Delicious at Greytown, Wairarapa, and introduced here in about 1932. They only do well in the south because they need reliable, sunny, autumn weather to ripen well. The conspicuous russeting is heavier in some districts than others and this makes them easier to distinguish amongst the confusion of Cox relatives. As well as the russeting, the stalk angle to the base can be distinctive and it is usually stout. The base hue is pale green, ripening to lemon-yellow, flushed with a deep orange-scarlet. There are short, dark red stripes and the lenticel dots are rather hidden as light spots.

The firm, juicy and sweet flesh is a deep cream colour. There is an excellent aromatic flavour. The blossom has been described as ornamental and has a similar look to the garden crab apple varieties. Like other triploid apples, the trees crop very well as long as there are two other pollinators. Little if any pruning is necessary. The pips are long, thin and pointed. The mid-green leaves look large and are sharply serrated, downy underneath.

Cox's Orange Pippin

dessert **J F** M A M J J A S **O N D**
medium round-conical
flowering group 3 freely spur-producing

group 7

The parent of so many of the world's finest apples, Richard Cox's famous fruit grew from the pip of a Ribston Pippin in Colnbrook Lawn, Slough, Buckingham-shire. First grown for the market by Thomas Rivers of Sawbridgeworth, Hertfordshire, in 1862 and voted the best dessert apple of the south in the 1883 RHS Apple Congress. Won its RHS First Class Certificate in 1962.

They do not like cold and wet years and thrive in warm, light situations. Queen Cox is a popular sport sold and the delicious flavour when the fruit has properly ripened is very aromatic and nutty. Neglected, shaded, trees develop canker and mildew, as happens on some soils. The flesh is creamy, firm, juicy and a little sweet. The fruit tends to be on the small size, but stores well.

Note the dry skin with a golden yellow base hue, flushed with orange and brown-red stripes. Lenticel spots show up as pale russet in the red areas. There is some russet at each end. The skin colour brightens with ripening. The stalk is of medium length and extends beyond the cavity. The blossom is a delicate pink and the leaves are yellow-green, pointed, bluntly serrated and rather thin and downy. As well as being the parent to many great apples, it is in season, itself, one of the greatest apples ever cultivated.

111

Jupiter

dessert **J F** M A M J J A S **O N D**
medium conical
flowering group 3 spur-bearing triploid

group 7

Cultivated by Dr F. Alston in 1966 at East Malling Research Station in Kent by crossing Cox's Orange Pippin with the more highly coloured Delicious sport, Starking Delicious. Named in 1973 and a commercial success, although Fiesta (Red Pippin) has less chewy skin and is more popularly grown now. The cropping is good from triploid pollination and they have a vigorous, spreading growth: suitable for the north. The flavour is intense, aromatic, sweet and juicy and the flesh creamy-white with rather coarse texture. Look for a pale green base colour which yellows and ripens to be flushed with the typical Cox family orange-red. Dark red stripes appear as a broken covering across the flush. Scarf skin, the russet tissue left after growth, shows round the base and surface of the apple. This can give a mottled effect to the skin surface. Lenticel dots show as specks surrounded by pale pink. Triploid.

The fruit is fairly symmetrical, but occasionally lop-sided. Faint ribs and crown. The stalk is often set at an angle to the cavity and is long, medium to stout. The pips look very thin and desiccated. There is a sweet aroma. The blossom is pale pink and the leaves are grey-green, upward folding and downy.

Ribston Pippin

dessert, cider J F M A M J J A S **O N** D
medium-large round-conical
flowering group 2 very freely spur-bearing triploid

group 7

The best loved dessert apple of the Victorian era and the long life of the original seedling indicates how old some apple trees can survive. Grown at Ribston Hall in about 1707 from a pip brought from France by Sir Henry Goodricke, Knaresborough, Yorkshire, the original tree died in 1835, but a shoot survived like a coppice stool and lived until 1932, having been blown over in 1928. As it was from a pip, the new tree would grow true to the original, but this does not, of course, happen with grafted trees where you just raise a root-stock from the soil, not the type. The fruit lasts until December, but is better earlier.

Taylor was very enthusiastic about its intense flavour and new research has shown it to be very high in vitamin C. The flesh is pale yellow, juicy, firm and also does well in cooking and cider production. Look for distinctly downy and fat fruit buds and haphazard russet patches on the apples which often cover the whole base round the stalk.

The stalk is itself noticeably short and below the top of the cavity. The pale green base colour yellows on ripening and the broken red stripes appear over an orange-brown flush. The lenticel spots show up best on the russet patches as green-brown spots. The blossom is very pale and pollination is triploid.

Leaves are oval, serrated, upward folding and mid-green, downy underneath.

113

Suntan

dessert **J F** M A M J J A S **O N D**
medium-large flat-round
flowering group 5 freely spur-bearing

 group 7

One of the brightest pink blossoms of all the Cox-related apples, Suntan was cultivated in 1955 by H.M. Tydeman at East Malling Research Station, Kent, by crossing Cox's Orange Pippin with Court Pendu Plat. Later flowering than Cox, it is useful in areas subject to frosts and it crops well. The trees are both vigorous and spreading. The fruit improves by December and keeps well into the new year. The skin is quite smooth and becomes a little greasy in storage. The base is flat with a hint of ribs. The flesh is deep cream, juicy, sweet-sharp (moderating with storage), aromatic, firm and of very good flavour. The base colour is pale green ripening to a golden yellow and the flush is orange-red, striped with crimson red. The lenticel spots show up clearly as little russet speckles and bumps.

There is usually russeting present, too. An attractive and symmetrical show variety. The pips look large and plump in the cell. The leaves are long, slender, large and upward-turning, bluntly serrated, dull green and very downy underneath. The stalk is short and stout.

Laxton's Superb

dessert J F M A M J J A S **O N** D
medium-large round-conical-conical
flowering group 4 spur-bearing

group 7

Cultivated from an early cross between Cox's Orange Pippin and Wyken Pippin by the Laxton Brothers at Bedford, 1897. It received the RHS Award of Merit in 1919 and a First Class Certificate in 1921. A flavour I have been able to enjoy fresh from old trees for over thirty years. This and other Laxton's types have been favourites through much of the last century. Noted for bearing fruit quickly, for being vigorous and for its heavy crops, with age it does become biennial. The taste will change from year to year, but in very sunny seasons it shows its Cox parentage in rich flavour. In fact it grows where Cox is poor and is suitable for the north. Look for what I think of as the 'Laxton purple' hue on a pale green–yellow base colour. Over the purple-red flush there are broken stripes and a light russeting appears at each end. The lenticel spots show as large russet spots. The fruit is brighter red in sunny years. The flesh is white, tinged green, crisp, juicy, refreshing.

Medium to long, stout stalk. The blossom is pale pink and the leaves are bright green to grey-green, upward folding, medium sized and serrated to varying degrees. They are downy underneath.

Rosemary Russet

dessert **J F M** A M J J A **S O N** D
medium conical
flowering group 3 freely spur-bearing

 group 7

Taylor called it 'More of a reinette than a russet' due to its red flush and only thin part-covering of russet. It is a highly prized dessert, but a little too small for the trade. Of unknown origin, it was described first by Ronalds of Brentford in Middlesex in 1831. The fruit can fall early, but the tree is a good, hardy cropper. The flesh is cream with a sweet-sharp, aromatic flavour. Look for a greenish-yellow base hue which yellows with ripening, a bright red-brown flush and some deep purple-red striping. The russet mottles the dry skin with a thin, pale brown covering and the lenticel spots show up as large russet dots. The stalk is long and stout.

Rather irregular in shape, like Sturmer Pippin (p.23) and frequently flat-sided. It is distinctly ribbed at the base. The blossom is intensely pink and we find it very ornamental in the garden. The dark green leaves are narrow and long, serrated, flat and slightly upward folding. The underside is only a little downy.

Bess Pool

dessert **J F** M A M J J A S **O N D**
medium round-conical
flowering group 6 mostly tip-bearing

This apple was discovered during the 1700s by Bess Pool, the daughter of an innkeeper, when she was walking in a wood in Nottinghamshire. Bunyard noted: 'A good old sort, keeping firm and crisp to the last'. He was, of course, referring to the excellent storage quality, rather than Bess Pool herself. It was already known by her name by 1802 and listed by Pearson, a Nottinghamshire nurseryman, by 1824. It is slow to come into bearing, which confines it to being a richly flavoured garden variety, but its very late flowering helps it resist frosts and it is suitable for valley sites which are prone to this problem. Irregular in shape, with indistinct ribs, there is a tendency for the fruit to have flat sides and be level at the top and bottom. The base colour is a dull grass-green and this yellows as it ripens. The flush is a dark purple-red with the lenticel dots picked out by reddening round the light spots. There are small patches of russet.

The flesh is white, sweetly scented, dry, with a pleasant flavour. Look for the short and stout stalk, which often has a lump at the point of joining with the branch on the tree. It has a strong pink blossom and narrow, mid-green, finely serrated leaves. They are not very downy underneath.

117

Adam's Pearmain

dessert **J F M** A M J J A S **O N D**
medium conical-long-conical
flowering group 2 partial tip-bearers

 group 7

The shape and lenticel speckles always make Robert Adam's superb apple easy to recognise and the flavour is excellent. It was called 'Norfolk Pippin' by Adam in 1826 and was also exhibited in Herefordshire as Hanging Pearmain. Hogg thought it to be a Herefordshire apple. (Just as I once thought Newton Wonder referred to Sir Isaac Newton, I thought this type was named after Adam in the Bible, neither of which is the case.) Hardy and scab resistant, they grow well in the west and tolerate late frosts. The rich, juicy and nutty taste is distinct and all I can think of to say against it might be the tough skin, although that is not a disadvantage for a tree in our climate. The flesh is pale yellow, a little sweet, and fine textured. They grow well in pots in gardens and have ornamental pale pink blossom. The apples are attractive for display and shows. The pear-shape is very obvious in many specimens and they tend to be lop-sided. The dull green base colour turns golden in ripening and the flush changes from brown-red to scarlet. There are short, broken red stripes with pale yellow lenticel dots. The skin is smooth and dry. The stalk is variable, medium to long. The leaves are small, oval, serrated, mid–green and downy.

Pixie
dessert **J F M** A M J J A S **O** N **D**
medium flat-round
flowering group 4 spur-bearing

group 7

This apple is thought to have been a Cox's Orange Pippin or a Sunset seedling grown in the RHS grounds at Wisley, Surrey, in 1947. It received the RHS Award of Merit in 1970 and their First Class Certificate in 1972. Despite their name, these apples achieve a medium size on well pruned trees, but are generally not large enough to market commercially. In an age of absurd regulations which restrict sales of such excellent fruit (yet seek miniature gadgets of every kind to increase commercial success in just about every other field) these very late keeping, refreshing apples are therefore suited only to gardens or farmers' markets. We dwarf our trees. Why not our fruit? The creamy flesh is tinged green near the core, with a juicy, sweet–sharp, intense and aromatic flavour and a crisp texture. The colourful fruit is of regular shape and there are no ribs. They are flat top and bottom. The stalk is characteristic as well, being long and quite thin. Small fruit on old trees might confuse, but this variety is not likely in very early established orchards planted before the 1950s.

The base colour is bright green, which yellows, flushed with orange-red. It has short, broken red stripes. The pale russet lenticel spots show up quite well. There is an attractive ornamental bright pink

blossom, which make it ideal for a garden with a young family. The leaves are light grass-green and bluntly serrated. They appear rather long compared with the fruit and are downy underneath.

119

Claygate Pearmain

dessert **J F** M A M J J A S **O** N **D**
medium large flat-round
flowering group 4   partial tip-bearer

 group 7

Taylor notes that its flavour is best in January and rather like Ribston Pippin, (p.113). It was found by John Braddick in 1821 in a hedge on the Firs Estate at Claygate in Surrey. In 1901 it received the RHS Award of Merit and later their First Class Certificate in 1921. It is a heavy cropper from a fairly vigorous tree that has been described as a tall Blenheim Orange. It has also been found to do well in garden pot culture on dwarfing rootstock. Look for a dull green base colour which yellows as it ripens. A brick-red flush develops which deepens to orange-red and there are broad broken stripes. The grey-brown russet gives the dry skin a rough feel and the lenticel spots show up as pale green or russet. The stalk is short and fairly stout.

These apples need exposure to prolonged sunshine to ripen really well. The flesh is white, tinged green and there is a rich, aromatic, nutty flavour. It is also sweet and juicy. They are flattened top and tail and there is a trace of ribs. The blossom is light pink and the leaves are mid-green. They are of medium size, broad and deeply serrated. They fold upward slightly and are very downy underneath.

Cornish Gilliflower

dessert **J F M** A M J J A S **O N D**

medium-large oblong-oblong-conical
flowering group 4 tip-bearing

group 7

As its name suggests, this very old variety does well in mild, wet conditions and, although it is a shy bearer, it was thought by Lindley in 1830 to be: 'the best apple that is known, if high flavour combined with a very rich sub–acid saccharine juice be the qualities we most desire in fruit...' Found in a cottage garden in Truro, Cornwall, about 1800, it was shown at the RHS in London in 1813 by Sir Christopher Hawkins and awarded their Silver Medal. Hogg linked the clove-like fragrance of the cut fruit with the old French word for clove, 'girofle', as being the source of the name.

Look for the distinct five-crowned ribs at the base which can be a little waisted. There is a very large core cell and slender stalk. The dull green base colour ripens to golden yellow, flushed with orange-red and bright red stripes. There are very obvious grey lenticel dots.

The skin is rough and dry, often with russet patches. The flesh is yellow, but shows as orange beneath the skin and is tinged green around the core. Flavour is sweet, rich and aromatic and texture is firm. It needs mild winters and a warm location. Bultitude notes that it 'cannot be grown in restricted form'. The blossom is a bright pink and the leaves are small, narrow and bluish-green. They are bluntly serrated, thin, upward-folding and downy.

Court Pendu Plat

dessert **J F M A** M J J A S **O** N **D**
medium flat
flowering group 6 freely spur-bearing

 group 7

Taylor thought this to probably be the oldest known type we grow in this country. It does well in modern pot culture and a number of special features are worthy of note: it has an exceptionally short stalk (named after 'short hanging' rather than a French Court, in 1540); very late flowering (given the old name Wise Apple because it missed late frosts as a result) and ornamental. The tree might be more successful nowadays if called Wise Apple, but it has probably survived since Roman times and the flavour is rich, aromatic and fruity. It keeps to the following spring and still has a pineapple-like tang into February. It looks rather like a Cox's Orange Pippin flattened at the top and bottom and has creamy-white flesh.

The fruits are well rounded with traces of ribs and crown at the apex. The trees are resistant to scab and hardy, with moderate growth.

Note the pale green-yellow hue, yellowing as it ripens and flushed with deep orange-red. There are red, broken stripes and russet spots round the lenticels. The skin is dry, usually with a russet patch round the stalk. It has a mid pink blossom, with grey-green, small leaves, upward folding and downy.

Barnack Beauty

dessert/dual **J F M** A M J J A **S** O N **D**
medium round-oval
flowering group 4 tip-bearing

group 7

A fine old dessert apple that also cooks well, from Barnack, Northamptonshire. Cultivated in a garden owned by a Mr Charles, it was commercially grown by W. & J. Brown of Stamford in about 1870. Received the RHS Award of Merit in 1899 and their First Class Certificate in 1909. Principally a garden variety and likely to be found in old orchard collections. Look for a very spreading tree, shiny fruit with a dry, bumpy surface to the pale green skin which yellows with ripening. The flush is a bright orange-red and the shape is symmetrical, only occasionally lop-sided: a 'true oval shape, regular in outline' as Taylor described one. Like Gascoyne's Scarlet (p.80) it is an important type if you: (a) live in a chalk district; (b) want a beautiful show apple and (c) enjoy ornamental, subtle, pink blossom. The creamy flesh is tinged orange, firm, juicy, sharp-sweet and crunchy.

There is some russeting top and bottom on the fruit and you can feel the small lenticel russet spots by touch. The leaves are mid-green, narrow, serrated and thin. There is a light grey down underneath.

Lord Hindlip

dessert **J F M** A M J J A S **O** N **D**
medium large conical-long-conical
flowering group 3   freely spur-bearing

 group 7

Before we had apples in our supermarkets all the year round very late dessert apples such as this were important to keep supplies going well into the following spring. If the apples also had 'show quality' looks, so much the better and this certainly applies to Lord Hindlip. It was cultivated in Worcestershire and is very resistant to scab. The first record is for 1896 and it was introduced by Watkins of Hereford and received the RHS Award of Merit that year. In 1898 it further gained the RHS First Class Certificate and became particularly popular as a garden variety in the West Midlands where it is still to be found. The trees are light-to-good croppers and the fruit makes a bright red, shiny exhibition variety. Look for the distinctly conical shape and angular ribbing, a dominant one making the apple rather lop-sided. The base colour is pale green, yellowing as it ripens, and the flush is a deep crimson. The russet varies and is netted across most of the fruit. The lenticel dots are small and grey.

The flesh is deep cream, firm, crisp, juicy and aromatic. The stalk is short and thick. There is bright, decorative, pink blossom and the leaves are small and narrow. They are mid to light green, markedly upward folding and very downy underneath.

Belle de Boskoop

dual, cider **J F M A** M J J A S **O** N **D**
medium large round-conical
flowering group 3 freely spur-bearing triploid

group 7

Found in Holland by K.J.W. Ottolander in 1856 and now a popular fruit grown commercially in Europe. Ottolander is said to have grafted from a Reinette de Montfort bud sport which attracted him by the fruit's colour and size. I find it very showy at blossom time and it is a handsome russet at harvest which also makes a good cider. The flesh is creamy, with green tinge, and flavour is slightly sweet. Cooks to a golden yellow and has a good, brisk flavour rather like Blenheim Orange. Received the RHS Award of Merit in 1897. Look for a green-yellow base colour which yellows to gold. It becomes flushed with a brick-red and orange-red stripes, although the dry skin is patched and netted with pale brown russet. The stalk is medium, sometimes above the cavity. There is a slight ribbing and the fruit is often lop-sided. Look out for it in Holland as Schone van Boskoop or Goudrenet.

The blossom is pale pink and it shares the prolific character of many triploid types: ample flowers and heavy cropping as long as pollination is good from two other trees. The leaves are medium to large, broad and oval with fine, sharp serrations. Their colour is light green and they are slightly upward turning at the edges. They are quite downy underneath.

125

Winston

dessert **J F M A** M J J A S **O** N **D**
medium-small round-conical-oblong-conical
flowering group 4 spur-bearing

group 7

Another Laxton Superb look-alike, due its Cox parentage, but smaller and more brightly coloured. The cross between Cox's Orange Pippin and Worcester Pearmain resulted in a later flowering type which stores well into the following spring. It was grown in 1920 by William Pope at Welford Park, Berkshire, and introduced in 1935 as Winter King. It was patriotically re-named Winston in 1944. Hardy and can be planted with late blossom types where frosts linger most. It is sweet with a strongly aromatic flavour. This mellows in storage. The skin is thick, but it also tolerates cool summers. The trees are heavy cropping from quite a vigorous tree. The flesh is creamy white and fine textured. Look for a greenish-yellow base colour and purple or orange-red flush. This can become a bright red and yellow-green contrast in storage. The stripes are broken red and fairly distinct. Sunshine makes the red a brighter hue. Smooth, dry skin and very faint ribbing.

Note the very stout stalk. The blossom is pale pink and the leaves are medium sized and angular with blunt serrations. They are sometimes downward folding (unusual in apples) and very downy.

Lord Burghley

dessert **J F M A** M J J A S **O** N D
small-medium round-slightly conical
flowering group 4 spur-bearing

group 7

Kept from being lost on waste ground in the gardens of the Marquis of Exeter by his head gardener, Mr Matheson, it is one of the latest dessert apples to come into season. The early writers recorded that it first bore fruit about 1834 and was one of the best winter dessert apples. It was raised at Burghley, Stamford, Lincolnshire. Introduced in 1865 and received the RHS First Class Certificate in that year. Because the fruit kept until May it was ideal for late storage before refrigeration and chilled imports allowed us to enjoy apples easily all the year round. It is ornamental and crops well in the garden with a rich, sweet-sharp and aromatic taste.

The flesh is white, tinged green, very firm and juicy. Look for the very obvious lenticel spots which show up on both the green-yellow base colour, and the red flush, as large russet dots. The apples become bright yellow and red later in storage.

Fairly vigorous and upward spreading, the trees produce small, intense pink blossom and the fruit hue is crimson-orange with faint streaks of red. The apple shape is flattened at the base and apex, a little flat-sided and ribbed. The stalk extends just beyond the fruit cavity and is stout. The leaves are oval, mid-green, bluntly serrated and only slightly upward folding. They are very downy underneath.

Tydeman's Late Orange

dessert **J F M A** M J J A S **O** N D
medium-small conical
flowering group 4 freely spur-bearing

group 7

Cox 'double-cross' by H.M. Tydeman at the East Malling Research Station Maidstone, Kent, in 1930, by using Cox's Orange Pippin and Laxton's Superb, which was itself of Cox parentage (with Wyken Pippin). A late to very late dessert, it was introduced in 1949 and was given the RHS Award of Merit in 1965. You may confuse it with Laxton Superb in looks, (p.115), but it has a season that lasts three months longer than Superb.

It does best in dry areas and the skin is slightly tougher than Superb. The flavour is just as good, with creamy white flesh, sweet-sharp, crisp and juicy. The apples are richly aromatic even before they are consumed.

Note that the stalk is usually longer than in Superb: medium to long and stout. The base colour is grass-green, ripening to yellow and flushed with the 'Laxton purple' hue (as I like to think of it). There are patches of grey brown russet and the lenticel spots show up quite well amongst the russeting. It has mid-pink blossom and light grey-green serrated leaves, slightly downy underneath.

GROUP 8
Saint Edmund's Pippin
dessert, cider J F M A M J J A **S O** N D
medium flat-round - round-conical
flowering group 2 freely spur-bearing

Bunyard considered this to be 'quite the best early russet' (and this is the first of the russets in this book). It was raised about 1875 by R. Harvey at Bury St Edmund's in Suffolk and named after the town's saint. It received an RHS First Class Certificate that year. Although it does not keep long and bruises easily, when it is fully ripe it has a sweet/sharp, nutty, juicy flavour. Like all russets (which are so often sold hard and green), it should not be eaten until it is fully ripe. The flesh is creamy white and it makes a good juice and cider, too. The stalk is fairly long and slender.

Look for the pale green–yellow base hue which turns golden. Some sunny-side fruits flush orange-red and there is a total russet covering which makes the lenticel spots faint. The skin is dry and a little rough. The shape is fairly regularly round, but sometimes lop-sided and flattened top and tail. They might over-crop and it is worth thinning the fruit for larger apples. The blossom is pale pink and the leaves are mid-green, medium size, oval, bluntly serrated and can be slightly upward-folding. The underside is only slightly downy.

Egremont Russet

dessert J F M A M J J A **S O N D**
medium flat-round
flowering group 2 very freely spur-bearing

 group 8

Recorded by J. Scott, Merriott, Somerset, 1872, and first exhibited in Dorset in 1883. Nothing known of its history otherwise. Morgan & Richards point out that the apple's name suggests that it arose on Lord Egremont's estate at Petworth in Sussex. The head gardener there maintained that this was so, but it is not listed in the estate records. It has become the most popular russet sold, but is picked too early for my tastes and should be ripened better. Fruit from our own garden tree brings out the nutty russet taste which is very distinctive. (The tree also came from Scott's Nursery). The flesh is creamy with a yellow tinge, aromatic, firm and juicy. Later this dries out and the flavour matures to what has been described as a 'tannic' quality.

Look for a base colour of green-yellow to the thick, dry skin, which ripens to golden yellow. There are no stripes, but the flush is an attractive brownish-orange, covered by ochre russet. The lenticel dots are obvious as light spots.

The stalk is very short and medium slender. The tree has an attractive pale pink blossom and has medium-sized leaves which are sharply and broadly serrated. They are thin, mid-green and slightly downy on the underside.

D'Arcy Spice

dessert **J F M A** M J J A S **O N D**
medium large oblong
flowering group 4 fairly freely spur-bearing

group 8

I was introduced to this excellent Essex apple by a kind villager at Little Berkhamsted who leaves a box of their garden surplus outside their gate. Friends convey them to us for Apple Day (21 October), although they are by tradition picked around Guy Fawkes, 5 November. The apple was found in the garden of The Hall, Tolleshunt d'Arcy about 1785, but probably has earlier origins. John Harris, nurseryman, introduced it as Baddow Pippin in 1848 after the location of the nursery, near Chelmsford. Noted for its keeping qualities and the development of a nutmeg flavour by January.

The flesh is white with a tinge of green like most russets. It is sweet-sharp, juicy, spicy (hence the title), and prefers a sunny autumn after a cool summer. Although the apple softens by May it is still very pleasant. If carefully stored, the skin does not shrivel. The stalk is short and stout - another feature of russets.

The blossom is a subtle pink and the leaves are medium-large and pointed. They are mid-green and some are downward folding. (Most apple leaves turn upwards slightly.) Downy underneath.

131

Nonpareil

dessert **J F M** A M J J A S **O N** D
medium-small round-conical
flowering group 5 freely spur-bearing

 group 8

Taylor reported only a few trees still survived by the 1930s and Bultitude considered it primarily for the connoisseur, grown in the garden. First recorded 1696 and thought to have been introduced from France. ('Nonpareil' means someone or something that is unsurpassed.) The sweet-sharp, aromatic, flavour is highly prized.

A weak, spreading tree which crops very well and is more available now. The fruit hangs late and sharpness is reduced by ample autumn sunshine. Look for a stout, long, thick-ended stalk and a well rounded shape to the fruit. The base colour is a light green, ripening to a yellow-green and there is a rusty-brown flush, often with some purple spots. The lenticel dots show up quite well as little pale russet lumps. There is also a light netting of russet top and tail which gives the dry skin a slightly rough feel. The creamy flesh is tinged green, with a juicy, fruity taste and firm texture.

The blossom is a subtle pink and the leaves are grey-green, bluntly serrated and slightly upward folding. They are flat to the touch rather than undulating and slightly downy underneath.

Ashmead's Kernel

dessert, cider **J F** M A M J J A S **O** N D
medium flat-round
flowering group 4 freely spur-bearing

group 8

I recall the great Harry Baker, who demonstrated grafting so well in the RHS Gardens at Wisley, saying that this was his top favourite amongst dessert apples. He was responsible for all the fruit, and must have tested more types than most of us ever see in our lifetimes.

I have found the trees slow to bear and it is important to keep the fruit for a month or so, but they have a juicy, sweet-sharp, richly aromatic flavour. The type was raised by Dr Ashmead in West Gloucestershire in about 1700 and due to its bland looks and uncertain cropping, took 150 years to be widely planted. The fine brown russet covers much of the grass-green base colour and there is often a light ochre-red flush with stripes.

Look for flat sides as well as the frequently lop-sided shape. The stalks are usually very short and stout. Because most of our own orchard apple pollen is in flowering group 3 and these are 4, I planted several in a group to help with their pollination. The blossom is an ornamental bright pink and the leaves are broad, mid-dark green, serrated and downy underneath. The apples also make a good cider.

Brownlees' Russet

dessert **J F M** A M J J A S **O N D**
medium large flat-round-slight conical
flowering group 4 very freely spur-bearing

 group 8

Taylor described these as a 'favourite russet for the private gardener' and they have an ornamental pink blossom which is particularly attractive. They were introduced by William Brownlees of Hemel Hempstead, Hertfordshire, about 1848. The flavour is firm, juicy, nutty and aromatic. We also cook them. Like all apples, but russets especially, wait until they are really ripe (from about December in this case) before you eat them as a dessert.

They crop well from a fairly vigorous tree, although some are rather erratic, possibly due to pollination problems and where they are sited. The base colour is a grassy green and dry skin is almost covered by a thin pale brown russet. The lenticel spots show up well as white russet spots, especially round the stalk. The very short stalk is medium thick and often has a lump near the end. The apple's shape is rather irregular. There are rounded ribs, flattened in the cavity round the stalk. The flesh is white, tinged green with a sweet flavour. The leaves are small, long, narrow and bluntly serrated, dark green and fairly downy underneath.

Duke of Devonshire

dessert **J F M** A M J J A S **O** N D
medium flat-round-round conical
flowering group 4 spur-bearing

group 8

Bunyard described it as 'quite indispens-able for late use' and it certainly keeps well into the spring. It was cultivated in 1835 by Mr Wilson, the Duke of Devonshire's gardener, at Holker Hall, Lancashire (Cumbria) and introduced in about 1875.

It is hardy, resistant to scab and copes with the higher rainfalls in the West Country. The trees are fairly vigorous and spreading, with rather light crops which tend to drop as they ripen. They can be flattened top and tail, sometimes lop-sided and have a round look. The dry skin is distinctive with a camouflage green ripening to a golden yellow. The sunny side occasionally produces a more brownish flush. There is a patchy netting of russet and the lenticel spots show up very well as white flecking. The flesh is cream, tinged green, firm, juicy, sweet-sharp, with a good nutty flavour. The stalk is extremely short and stout.

The blossom is very pale pink and the leaves are dark green and pointed, bluntly serrated, medium thick and very downy underneath.

Growing in popularity

The following types are growing in popularity and are given a brief summary:

Alkmene

dessert  *group 7*

J F M A M J J A **S O** N D

large round flowering group 2

A crisp and juicy German variety cultivated by Prof. M. Schmidt during the 1930s. It was the result of a cross between Dr Oldenburg and Cox's Orange Pippin. They ripen before Cox, however, and have become widely grown throughout Germany and Holland. There is a honey flavour and they are aromatic. Their season is shorter than that of the parent Cox. Introduced in 1972, but not widely available from nurseries here yet. Stocked by Deacon's Nursery. Also known as Early Windsor.

Braeburn *group 4*

dessert

J F M A M J J A S **O** N D

large round flowering group 2

A popular juicy New Zealand apple with excellent flavour. They are a feature of our supermarkets now and although they have had problems with fully ripening here, it is likely that our climate will suit them increasingly. A seedling, it is thought, of Lady Hamilton and it handles well without easily bruising. Popular as a commercial crop in France and the United States as well as New Zealand. Flushed with a smooth skin; flesh crisp and juicy. Trees need a light, sunny location.

Elstar

group 4 dessert

J F M A M J J A S **O N D**

medium round
flowering group 2

One of the best Dutch dessert apples and the result of a cross between Ingrid Marie and Golden Delicious introduced in 1972. They are now becoming available from major nurseries and are sold in some supermarkets. We have found them to be popular when put on display and tasted at our Apple Day event, too. Now grown throughout Europe, but said to have poor colour in England, although I have not noticed this myself. They are heavy cropping and store well. There is a red flush and stripes with some russet around the long, thin stalk.

Princess

group 8 dessert

J F M A M J J A S **S** O N D

medium oblong
flowering group 2

A recently introduced russet from France that grows strongly and has an excellent nutty flavour. Known as Reine du Reinette (King of the Pippins) it has, however, earlier blossom and will probably become known as Princess. Frank P. Matthews Nursery report them to be easier to grow than Egremont Russet and heavy cropping. King of the Pippins. p.109, has only thin russet on the skin in comparison and looks quite different.

Red Falstaff

dessert  *group 4*

J F M A M J J A S **O N D**

large round-oblong
flowering group 2

The popular red sport of Falstaff
cultivated by Dr F. Alston in Kent by
crossing James Grieve with Golden
Delicious in 1965 and introduced in
1986. With the same red countenance
as the Shakespearian character after
which it was named, it has proved frost
resistant and a good pollinator for other
apples nearby. They are crisp, juicy and
heavy cropping. They also store well and
may last well beyond December. There
are stripes as well as the red flush.

The fairly recent Australian cross
between Golden Delicious and Lady
Williams, called Pink Lady, is similar in
size with a pale green area around the
stalk. It is uncertain how this all-purpose
apple will ripen in Britain, but the
imported fruit has a pleasant mild flavour
with good aroma and is widely available
in the shops now.

Red Windsor

dessert  *group 6*

J F M A M J J A **S O** N D

medium round
flowering group 2

An attractive red sport of Alkmene from
Hereford in 1985. Alkmene, shown on
p.136, is known as Early Windsor. It
retains a strong Cox flavour and crops
heavily. Rich, crisp and aromatic. The
tree grows with moderate vigour and
has resistance to frost. With such juicy
and prolific fruit it is therefore an ideal
variety for the garden.

Scrumptious

group 6 🍎 dessert

J F M A M J J A **S O** N D

medium round

flowering group 3

The Frank P. Matthews Nursery consider this a very special dessert cultivated specifically for the garden conditions in Britain. It is an example of a type developed and protected by the *Plant Breeders Rights* and propagation is possible only by licence. This form of copyright is administered at Brogdale and you must not, for example, graft from these trees to sell them without payment to the licence holder. They are self-fertile, frost-hardy, disease resistant and bright red with some striping. They are ideal straight from the tree during September, but will last to the end of October in cool conditions. They have a good aroma and are crisp and sweet.

Winter Gem

group 4 🍎

dessert

J F M A M J J A S **O N D**

medium round

flowering group 2

Another recent introduction, raised originally in 1977 from a cross between Cox's Orange Pippin and Grimes Gold, it was voted the best plate of apples at the RHS London show in 1999. Heavy cropping, excellent flavour with a firm and crisp texture. Store well until spring from the October picking. Pale green stripes obvious amongst the red flush and streaks. Distinct five crown bumps. Attractive pale pink blossom.

3 What are your local apple varieties?

THE COMPREHENSIVE *FRUIT & VEG FINDER*, published by the Henry Doubleday Research Association with the help of Brogdale Horticultural Trust gives a guide to apple varieties by county to help growers who wish to preserve varieties of local interest.

I strongly recommend the purchase of this guide for the range of fruit and vegetables covered. Pears and plums are listed in the book and you can also trace the history of potatoes, for example.

A much extended county list, also including apples from Ireland, Scotland and Wales, with descriptions mixed in for favourite types has also been published in *The Common Ground Book of Orchards* (2000). The authors point out that if you seek your local varieties to grow they are more likely to suit your local soil and weather conditions.

Many of the varieties listed below are found in the National Fruit Collection at Brogdale which is in Faversham, Kent, and they help propagate types you may be interested in. I have based the following list on the *Finder*, books on cider apples and Common Ground's lists with a few corrections and additions from my own experience, but it has to just be a general guide and is not intended to be definitive. Many are featured in this book, but there are some very local types with endearing names which you may only find now at Brogdale or in orchards local to the areas listed. The varieties, with their often historic names, are also shown in alphabetical order, dessert and dual purpose, cooking, cider and crab starting on pp. 146–154.

Always contact Brogdale first before you visit and join the Friends of Brogdale if you are likely to be a regular visitor. They have a full programme of events through the year and regular newsletters to let you know what is going on.

Avon and Somerset

Ashton Bitter, Ashton Brown Jersey, Backwell Red, Bailbrook Seedling, Bartletts Glory, Bath Russet, Beauty of Bath, Beauty of Blackmoor, Beauty of Wells, Black Dabinett, Black Vallis, Bridgewater Pippin, Broadleaf Jersey, Brockhead, Burrowhill Early, Cap of Liberty, Camelot, Cheddar Cross, Chisel Jersey, Coat Jersey, Cooper's Favourite, Court of Wick, Crimson King, Dabinett, Dorset, Dove, Dunning's Russet, Even Pearmain, Exeter Cross, Fair Maid of Taunton, Fillbarrel, Gatcombe, Glory of the West, Gloucester Cross, Golden Farmer, Golden Knob, Greasy Pippin, Green Pearmain, Hagloe Pippin, Harry Masters Jersey, Hereford Cross, Hoary Morning, Kingston Black, Lambrook Pippin, Lambrook Seedling, Loddington, Maggie Grieve, Mealy Late Blossom, Melmoth, Merchant Apple, Newport Cross, Nine Square, Pennard Bitter, Plymouth Cross, Poor Man's Profit, Porter's Perfection, Puffin, Pyleigh, Radcliffe Nonpareil, Red Worthy, Rich's Favourite, Rough Pippin, St Ivel Pippin, Shoreditch White, Somerset Lasting, Stable Jersey, Stembridge Cluster, Stembridge Jersey, Stoke Red, Taunton Cross, Taunton Golden Pippin, Taunton Nonpareil, Taylor's Sweet, Tom Putt, White Close Pippin, White Jersey, Worcester Cross, Yarlington Mill, Yeovil Sour

Bedfordshire

Advance (also known as Laxton's Advance), Ballard Beauty, Beauty of Bedford, Bedfordshire Foundling, Duchess of Bedford, Epicure, Exquisite, Hambling's Seedling, Laxton's Early Crimson, Laxton's Favourite, Laxton's Fortune, Laxton's Herald, Laxton's Leader, Laxton's Pearmain, Laxton's Peerless, Laxton's Rearguard, Laxton's Reward, Laxton's Royalty, Laxton's Superb, Laxton's Triumph, Laxton's Victory, Lord Lambourne, Neild's Drooper, Owen Thomas, Pioneer, Queenby's Glory, September Beauty

Berkshire

Breedon Pippin, Charles Eyre, Charles Ross, Delectable, Encore, Formosa Nonpareil, Frogmore Prolific, Guelph, Hector MacDonald, Houblon, John Standish, John Waterer, Miller's Seedling, Mrs Phillimore, Paroquet, Peacemaker, Renown, Rival, Shinfield Seedling, Small's Admirable, Sunrise, Welford Park Nonsuch, Winston

Buckinghamshire

Arthur Turner, Ball's Pippin, Cox's Orange Pippin, Cox's Pomona, Feltham Beauty, Langley Pippin, Small's Admirable, S T Wright

Cambridgeshire

Allington Pippin, Barnack Beauty, Chiver's Delight, Cottenham Seedling, Early Victoria (Emneth Early), Green Harvey, Haggerstone Pippin, Histon Favourite, Hunter's Majestic, Huntingdon Codlin, Lord Peckover, Lynn's Pippin, Morley's Seedling, Murfitt's Seedling, New Rock Pippin, Red Victoria, Saint Everard, Wayside

Cheshire

Arthur W Barnes, Bee Bench, Burr Knot, Celia, Eccleston Pippin, Elton Beauty, Gooseberry Pippin, Lord Clyde, Lord Derby, Millicent Barnes, Minshull Crab, Pott's Seedling, Rakemaker, Rymer, Shaw's Pippin, Sure Crop, Withington Welter

Cornwall

Ben's Red, Blackmoor Pippin, Bottlestopper, Box Apple, Bread Fruit, Captain Broad, Chacewater Longstem, Collogget Pippin, Cornish Aromatic, Cornish Gilliflower, Cornish Honeypin, Cornish Longstem, Cornish Mother, Cornish Pine, Fairfield (Millet), Glass Apple (Snell's White), Gulval Seedling, Hocking's Green, Hocking's Yellow, Hodge's Seedling, Improved Keswick, King Byerd, Manaccan Promise, Onion Moonstreak, Pear Apple, Pig's Nose, Pig's Snout, Plympton King, Polly (Whitehair), Queenie, Red Robin, Red Rollo, Sawpit, Scilly Pearl, Sidney Strake, Sops in Wine, Sweet Larks, Sweet Merlin, Tan Harvey, Tommy Knight, Tregonna King, Trenance Cooker, Venus Pippin

Cumbria

Autumn Harvest, Carlisle Codlin, Forty Shilling, Greenup's Pippin (Yorkshire Beauty), Keswick Codlin, Lemon Square, Longstart, Nelson's Favourite

Derbyshire

Beeley Pippin, Belledge Pippin, Lamb's Seedling, New Bess Pool, Newton Wonder

Devonshire

Allspice, Duke of Devonshire, Barum Beauty, Beech Bearer, Beef Apple, Bickington Grey, Billy Down Pippin, Bowden's Seedling, Brown's Apple, Butterbox, Cerit, Coleman's Seedling, Crimson Costard, Dawe, Devonshire Buckland, Devonshire Court Pendu, Devon Crimson Queen, Devonshire Quarrenden, Devonshire Redstreake, Devonshire Striped, Devonshire Whitesour, Docker's Devonshire, Ellis Bitter, Endsleigh Beauty, Fair Maid of Devon, Farmer's Glory, Golden Bittersweet, Hollow Core, Johnny Voun, Limberland, Lucombe's Pine, Lucombe's Seedling, Major, Michaelmas Stubbard, Morgan Sweet, No Pip, North Wood, Oaken Pin, Paignton Marigold, Peter Lock, Plympton Pippin, Ponsford, Pyne's Pearmain, Quench, Red Ribbed Greening, Royal Somerset, Slack Ma Girdle, Star of Devon, Stockbearer, Sweet Alford, Sweet Coppin, Tom Potter, Tremlett's Bitter, Upton Pyne, Veitch's Perfection, Whitesour, Woodbine, Woolbrook Pippin, Woolbrook Russet

Bramley blossom.

Dorset
Iron Pin, Melcombe Russet, Mollyanne, Tyneham Apple

Essex
Acme, Braintree Seedling, Chelmsford Wonder, D'Arcy Spice, Discovery, Edith Hopwood, Eros, Essex Pippin, Excelsior, Flame, Francis, Garnet, George Cave, London Pippin, Maclean's Favourite, Maldon Wonder, Monarch, Montfort, Morris's Russet, Opal, Pearl, Queen, Rosy Blenheim, Ruby, Seabrook's Red, Stanway Seedling, Stradbroke, Sturmer Pippin, Sunburn, Waltham Abbey Seedling

Gloucestershire
Ashmead's Kernel, Bedminster Pippin, Breakwell's Seedling, Bromsbury Crab, Chaxhill Red, Eden, Elmore Pippin, Forest Styre, Gilliflower of Gloucester, Gloucester Royal, Hunt's Duke of Gloucester, Lake's Kernel, Lodgemore Nonpareil, Longney Russet, Martin's Kernel, Morning Pippin, Must, Northland Seedling, Old Foxwhelp, Puckrup Pippin, Severn Bank, Tewkesbury Baron, Yellow Styre

Greater Manchester
Lord Suffield

Greater London and Middlesex
Barchard's Seedling, Cellini, Chad's Favourite, Fearn's Pippin, Grange's Pearmain, Hounslow Wonder, London Pearmain, Langley Pippin, Merton Beauty, Merton Charm, Merton Delight, Merton Joy, Merton Knave, Merton Pearmain, Merton Pippin, Merton Prolific, Merton Reinette, Merton Russet, Merton Worcester, Mitchelson's Seedling, Morris's Russet, Pinner Seedling, Reverend W. Wilks, Royal Jubilee, Scarlet Pearmain, Storey's Seedling

Hampshire and The Isle Of Wight
Beauty of Hants, Beneden Early, Bramshott Rectory, Deacon's Blushing Beauty, Deacon's Millennium, Easter Orange, Hambledon Deux Ans, Howgate Wonder, Isle of Wight Pippin, Isle of Wight Russet, James Saunders, Jersey Beauty, King George V, Lady Thornycroft, Lord Kitchener, Royal Snow, Sir John Thornycroft, Steyne's Seedling

Herefordshire
Adam's Pearmain, Ball's Bittersweet, Bringewood Pippin, Brown Snout, Cherry Pearmain, Cowarne Red, Downton Pippin, Forester, Golden Harvey, Herefordshire Beefing, King's Acre Bountiful, King's Acre Pippin, Lady's Finger of Hereford, New German, Pig's Nose Pippin, Pitmaston Pineapple, Redstreak, Stoke Edith Pippin, Strawberry Norman, Ten Commandments, Tyler's Kernel, Wormsley Pippin, Yellow Ingestrie

Hertfordshire

Beauty of Waltham, Brownlees' Russet, Bushey Grove, Dawn, Edwin Beckett, Fairie Queen, Golden Reinette, Gavin, Hitchin Pippin, Hormead Pearmain, Lane's Prince Albert, New Hawthornden, Prince Edward, River's Early Peach, River's Nonsuch, Riversii, Smiling Morn, St Martin's, Thomas Rivers, Voyager, Wilson's Endeavour, Winter Hawthornden, Young's Pinello

Huntingdonshire

Huntingdon Codlin

Ireland

Ard Cairn Russet, Ballinora Pippin, Balleyfatten, Barnhill Pippin, Bloody Butcher, Brown Crofton, Clearheart, Dockney, Dunkitt, Ecklinville, Eight Square, Farrell, Gibbon's Russet, Gibby's Apple, Golden Royal, Greasy Pippin, Green Chisel, Honey Ball, Irish Peach, Keegan's Crab, Kemp, Kerry Pippin, Kilkenny Pearmain, Lady's Finger of Offaly, Martin's Seedling, Munster Tulip, Pêche Melba, Reid's Seedling, Richardson, Ross Nonpareil, Sam Young, Scarlet Crofton, Sovereign, Striped Brandy, Striped Sax, Strippy, Summer John, Thompson's Apple, Tommy, Valentine, White Russet, Widow's Friend, Yellow Pitcher

Isle of Man

Manks Codlin

Kent

Bascombe's Mystery, Beauty of Kent, Bolero, Bountiful, Bow Hill Pippin, Brenchley Pippin, Castle Major, Chips, Christmas Pearmain, Cobham, Colonel Vaughan, Cooper's Seedling, Diamond Jubilee, Falstaff, Faversham Creek, Fiesta, Folkestone, Foster's Seedling, Fred Webb, Gascoyne's Scarlet, George Neal, Golden Knob, Gooseberry, Granny Giffard, Great Expectations, Greensleeves, Grenadier, Jester, Jupiter, Kent, Kentish Fillbasket, Kentish Quarrenden, Lamb Abbey Pearmain, Lily Boxall, Mabbott's Pearmain, Maid of Kent, Maidstone Favourite, Michaelmas Red, Orange Goff, Polka, Polly Prosser, Red Devil, Redsleeves, Robin Pippin, Rossie Pippin, St Albans Pippin, Smart's Prince Arthur, South Park, Sunset, Suntan, Tydeman's Early, Tydeman's Late Orange, Wanstall Pippin, Warner's King, Waltz

Lancashire

Duke of Devonshire, Golden Spire, Gold Medal, Harvest Festival, Hutton Square, John Huggett, Lady's Finger of Lancaster, Lange's Perfection, Keswick Codlin, Pott's Seedling, Proctor's Seedling, Roseberry, Sowman's Seedling

Leicestershire and Rutland

Annie Elizabeth, Barnack Orange, Belvoir Seedling, Dumelow's Seedling (Wellington), Marriage Maker, Prince Charles, Queen Caroline, Saint Ailred

Lincolnshire

Allington Pippin, Barnack Beauty, Brown's Seedling, Dewdney's Seedling, Doctor Clifford, Ellison's Orange, Grimoldby Golden, Herring's Pippin, Holland Pippin, Ingall's Pippin, Ingall's Red, Isaac Newton's Tree, Lord Burghley, Peasgood's Nonsuch, Philadelphia, Schoolmaster, Sleeping Beauty, Uland, William Ingall

Merseyside

Florence Bennett

Sixty-year-old Bramley in blossom.

Norfolk
Adam's Pearmain, Admiral, Banns, Baxter's Pearmain, Beachamwell, Caroline, Dr Harvey, Foulden Pearmain, Golden Noble, Green Roland, Harling Hero, Harvey, Herbert Eastoe, Horsford Prolific, Horsham Russet, Hubbard's Pearmain, Norfolk Beauty, Norfolk Beefing, Norfolk Coleman, Norfolk Royal, Robert Blatchford, Norfolk Summer Broadend, St Magdalen, Sandringham, Striped Beefing, Vicar of Beighton, White Quarantine, Winter Broadend, Winter Majetin

Northamptonshire
Barnack Beauty, Eady's Magnum, Lord Burghley, Thorpe's Peach

Northumberland
Mrs Lakeman's Seedling

Nottinghamshire
Baron Ward, Beauty of Stoke, Bess Pool, Bramley's Seedling, Domino, Mead's Broading, Grantonian, Mrs Wilmot, Nottingham Pippin, Pickering's Seedling, Radford Beauty, Sisson's Workshop, Newtown, Winter Quarrenden

Oxfordshire
Blenheim Orange, Caudal Market, Corry's Wonder, Eynsham Challenger, Eynsham Dumpling, Foulke's Foremost, Hanwell Souring, Jennifer, Jennifer Wastie, Old Fred, Oxford Beauty, Oxford Conquest, Oxford Hoard, Oxford Sunrise, Oxford Yeoman, Peggy's Pride, Pheasant's Eye, Red Army, Redstart, Sergeant Peggy, Wardington Seedling

Scotland

Alderman, Arbroath Pippin, Beauty of Moray, Bloody Ploughman, Cambusnethan Pippin, Coul Blush, Cutler Grieve, Early Julyan, East Lothian Pippin, Galloway Pippin, Hawthornden, Hood's Supreme, James Grieve, Lady of the Lake, Lady of the Wemyss, Lass O'Gowrie, Lord Rosebery, Maggie Sinclair, Oslin, Pine Golden Pippin, Port Allen Russet, Scotch Bridget, Seaton House, Stirling Castle, Stobo Castle, Thomas Jeffrey, Thorle Pippin, Tower of Glamis, Warden, White Melrose, White Paradise

Shropshire

Bringewood Pippin, Brookes, Lady's Fingers, Moss's Seedling, Prince's Pippin, Springrove Codlin

Suffolk

Beachamwell, Catherine, Clopton Red, Honey Pippin, Lady Henniker, Lord Stradbroke, Maclean's Favourite, St Edmund's Pippin, Sturmer Pippin

Surrey

Albury Park Nonsuch, Braddick's Nonpareil, Byfleet Seedling, Carswell's Honeydew, Carswell's Orange, Claygate Pearmain, Cleeve, Cockle Pippin, Colonel Yate, Comrade, Curl Tail, Dalice, Duchess's Favourite, George Carpenter, Glebe Gold, Hannon Seedling, Harry Pring, High View Pippin, John Divers, Joybells, King of the Pippins, Lady Isabel, Margaret Taylor, Mary Green, May Beauty, Mitchelson's Seedling, Nanny, Palmer's Rosey, Pixie, Prince George, Scarlet Crofton, Scarlet Nonpareil, Shoesmith, Smiler, Surprise, Victory, Wadey's Seedling, William Peters, Ye Old Peasgood

Sussex

Aldwick Beauty, Alfriston, Ashdown Seedling, Coronation, Crawley Beauty, Crawley Reinette, Coronation, Doctor Hogg, Duck's Bill, Eastbourne Pippin, Edmund Jupp, Egremont Russet, First and Last, Forge, Golden Bounty, Golden Pippin, Hawkridge, June Crewdson, Knobby Russet, Lady Hopetown, Lady Sudeley, Mannington's Pearmain, Mareda, Old Middlemas, Petworth Nonpareil, Saltcote Pippin, Sussex Mother, Tinsley Quince, Wadhurst Pippin

Tyne & Wear

Barnard's Baker, Gateshead Lemon Pippin, Hebburn Red, Teesdale Nonpareil, Woolaton Pippin

Wales

Baker's Delicious, Breakwell's Seedling, Channel Beauty, Chaxhill Red, Cissy, Cummy Norman, Frederick, Monmouthshire Beauty, Saint Cecilia

Warwickshire

Hunt's Early, Shakespeare, Wyken Pippin

Wiltshire

Bedwyn Beauty, Burn's Seedling, Celt, Chorister Boy, Dredge's Fame, Mary Barnett, Roundway, Magnum Bonum

Worcestershire

Betty Geeson, Colwall Quoining, Dick's Favourite, Edward Vll, Gladstone, Green Purnell, Hope Cottage Seedling, King Charles Pearmain, Lord Hindlip, Madresfield Court, May Queen, Pitmaston Russet Nonpareil, Pitmaston Pineapple, Sandlin Duchess, Tupstones, Whiting Pippin, William Crump, Worcester Pearmain

Yorkshire

Acklam Russet, Cockpit, Fillingham Pippin, Flower of the Town, French Crab, Green Balsam, Greenups Pippin, Hunt House, Nursery Asses, Ribston Pippin, Sharleston Pippin, Syke House Russet (English Hospital Reinette), Yorkshire Greening

Alphabetical list of apples

I have selected the following 1,288 types planted in the British Isles which do well here, but the list includes many popular overseas varieties which suit our conditions, too. An extensive list including world types is given in Martin Crawford's excellent work of reference, *Directory of Apple Cultivars*. There is variation in the spelling of old types and the names in my copy of the *Hereford Pomona* have been edited into those used in more modern times where relevant. (I have also left out most of the chance variations in colour and other features known as 'sports' of well known varieties, unless they are very popular).

Key:

So as not to have separate alphabetical lists for the reader to search through I have set the dessert and dual purpose apples in roman type, *cooking apples* in italic, **cider apples** in bold and a few examples of ***crab apples*** in bold italic. This is, however, only a general guide: many are dual purpose and many not classified as cider apples make excellent cider too.

Acklam Russet
Acme
Adam's Pearmain
Admiral
Advance
Akars Seedling
Alastair Cannon-White
Albury Park Nonsuch
Aldenham Blenheim
Aldenham Purple
Alderman
Aldwick Beauty
Alexander Dean
Alexis
Alfriston
Alkmene
Allen's Everlasting
Allington Pippin
Allspice
Alnarp's Favourite
Anna
Anna Boelens
Annie Elizabeth
Api Noir
Arbroath Pippin
Archimedes
Ard Cairn Russet
Aromatic Russet
Arthur Sheen
Arthur Turner

Arthur W. Barnes
Ascot
Ashdown Seedling
Ashmead's Kernel
Ashton Bitter
Ashton Brown Jersey
Autumn Harvest
Autumn Pearmain
Backwell Red
Bailbrook Seedling
Bailey's Record
Baker's Delicious
Ballard Beauty
Ballinora Pippin
Ball's Bittersweet
Ball's Pippin
Ballyfatten
Banns
Barchard's Seedling
Barnack Beauty
Barnack Orange
Barnard's Baker
Barnhill Pippin
Baron Ward
Baron Wood
Bartlett's Glory
Barton
Barum Beauty
Bascombe Mystery
Bath Russet

Baumann's Reinette
Baxter's Pearmain
Bazeley
Beachamwell (Paton)
Beachamwell (Tatham)
Beauty of Bath
Beauty of Bedford
Beauty of Blackmoor
Beauty of Hants
Beauty of Kent
Beauty of Moray
Beauty of Stoke
Beauty of Waltham
Beauty of Wells
Bedfordshire Foundling
Bedminster Pippin
Bedwyn Beauty
Bee Bench
Beech Bearer
Beef Apple
Beeley Pippin
Belgolden No 17
Bell Apple
Bellaqueeny
Belle Bonne
Belle de Boskoop
Belle de Pointoise
Belledge Pippin
Belvoir Seedling
Benenden Early

146

Ben's Red
Bess Pool
Best In England
Betsey
Betsy Baker
Betty Geeson
Bickington Grey
Billy Down Pippin
Bismarck
Black Dabinett
Blackmoor Pippin
Black Vallis
Bledisloe Cox
Blenheim Orange
Blood of the Boyne
Bloody Butcher
Bloody Ploughman
Blue Pearmain
Bodenham Beauty
Bolero
Bosbury Pippin
Bossom
Bottlestopper
Bountiful
Bovey
Bowden's Seedling
Bowhill Pippin
Box Apple
Braddick Nonpareil
Braeburn
Braeburn; Hilwell Strain
Braintree Seedling
Bramley's Seedling
Bramshott Rectory
Bread Fruit
Breakwell's Seedling
Breedon Pippin
Brenchley Pippin
Bridgwater Pippin
Brighton
Brimley Bittersweet
Bringewood Pippin
Broad End
Broad-Eyed Pippin
Broadleaf Jersey
Brock
Brockhead
Bromsbury Crab
Brookes's
Brown Crofton
Brown Kenting
Brownlees' Russet
Brown Snout

Brown Thorn
Brown's Apple
Brown's Seedling
Broxwood Foxwhelp
Bulmer's Foxwhelp
Bulmer's Norman
Burgess Seedling
Burn's Seedling
Burr Knot
Burrowhill Early
Burton Lemon
Bushey Grove
Butterbox
Buttery Door
Buxted Favourite
Byfleet Seedling
Byford Wonder
Cadbury
Calville Blanc D'Hiver
Cambusnethan Pippin
Camelot
Cap of Liberty
Captain Broad
Captain Kidd
Captain Tom
Cardross Green
Carlisle Codlin
Carlton
Carnation Rose
Caroline
Carswell's Honeydew
Carswell's Orange
Carter's Pearmain
Castle Major
Catherine
Catshead
Caudal Market
Cavallotta
Celia
Cellini
Celt
Cerit
Chacewater Longstem
Chad's Favourite
Channel Beauty
Chantry's Seedling
Charles Eyre
Charles Ross
Charlottae
Charlotte
Chatley's Kernel
Chaxhill Red
Cheddar Cross

Cheddar Pearmain
Chelan Red
Chelmsford Wonder
Cherry Pearmain
Chips
Chisel Jersey
Chiver's Delight
Chorister Boy
Christmas Pearmain
Churchill
Cider Lady's Finger
Cinderella
Cissy
Clarinette
Classic Red Delicious
Claygate Pearmain
Clearheart
Cleeve
Clemens
Climax
Clopton Red
Clydesdale
Coat Jersey
Cobham
Cockett's Red
Cockle Pippin
Cockpit
Coe's Golden Drop
Coeur de Boeuf
Coker Seedling
Coleman's Seedling
Collington Big Bitters
Collogget Pippin
Colonel Harboard's Pippin
Colonel Vaughan
Colonel Yate
Colwall Quoining
Comrade
Congresbury Beauty
Cooper's Favourite
Cooper's Seedling
Coo's River Beauty
Cornish Aromatic
Cornish Gilliflower
Cornish Honeypin
Cornish Longstem
Cornish Mother
Cornish Pine
Coronation
Corry's Wonder
Corse Hill
Costard Mainds
Costard Wotton

Cottenham Seedling
Coul Blush
Court of Wick
Court Pendu Plat
Court Royal
Cowarne Red
Cow's Snout
Cox Self Fertile
Cox's Orange Pippin
Cox's Pomona
Craggy's Seedling
Crawley Beauty
Crawley Reinette
Credenhill Pippin
Crimson Bramley
Crimson Custard
Crimson King
Crimson Newton Wonder
Crimson Peasgood
Crimson Queening
Crimson Spy
Crimson Superb
Crimson Victoria
Crispin
Crofton Scarlet
Crowned Pippin
Cummy Norman
Curl Tail
Cutler Grieve
Dabinette
Dalice
Daliter Elton
D'Arcy Spice
Dartmouth
Dawe
Dawn
Decio
Delbarestivale
Delectable
Desse de Buff
Devon Crimson Queen
Devonshire Buckland
Devonshire Court Pendu
Devonshire Red Streake
Devonshire Striped
Devonshire Quarrenden
Devonshire Whitesour
Dewdney's Seedling
Dewdulip Seedling
Diamond Jubilee
Diana
Dick's Favourite
Dillington Beauty

Discovery
Docker's Devonshire
Dockney
Doctor Clifford
Doctor Hogg
Domino
Dorset
Dove
Downton Pippin
Dredge's Fame
Dr Harvey
Duchess of Bedford
Duchess of Gloucester
Duchess of Oldenburg
Duchess's Favourite
Duck's Bill
Dudley
Dufflin
Duke of Devonshire
Dumelow's Seedling
(Wellington)
Dunkerton Late Sweet
Dunkitt
Dunn's Seedling
Dymock Red
Eady's Magnum
Earl Cowper
Early Julyan
Early Red Jersey
Early Victoria (Emneth Early)
Eastbourne Pippin
Easter Orange
East Lothian Pippin
Eccleston Pippin
Ecklinville
Eden
Edith
Edith Hopwood
Edmonds
Edmund Jupp
Edward V11
Edwin Beckett
Eggleton Styre
Egremont Russet
Eight Square
Ellis Bitter
Ellison's Orange
Elmore Pippin
Elstar
Elton Beauty
Emily Childs
Empire
Encore

Endsleigh Beauty
English Codlin
Epicure
Ernie's Russet Fortune
Eros
Esopus Spitzenburg
Essex Pippin
Evening Gold
Even Pearmain
Excelsior
Exeter Cross
Exquisite
Eynsham Challenger
Eynsham Dumpling
Fairfield
Fairie Queen
Fair Maid of Devon
Fair Maid of Taunton
Fairy
Fallbarrow Favourite
Falstaff
Farmer Jack
Farmer's Glory
Farmer's Seedling
Farrell
Faversham Creek
Fearn's Pippin
Feltham Beauty
Fenouillet Rouge
Fiesta (Red Pippin)
Fillbarrel
Fillingham Pippin
First and Last
Fisher Fortune
Fish's Pippin
Five Crowns
Flame
Flamenco
Fletcher's Prolific
Florence Bennett
Flower of the Town
Folkestone
Forester
Forest Styre
Forge
Formosa Nonpareil
Fortune (Laxton's)
Forty Shilling
Foster's Seedling
Foulden Pearmain
Foulkes' Foremost
Foxwhelp
Francis

Franklyn's Golden Pippin
Frederick
Fred Webb
French Crab
Frogmore Prolific
Fuji
Gabalva
Gala
Galloway Pippin
Garland's Long Keeper
Garnet
Gascoyne's Scarlet
Gateshead Lemon Pippin
Gatcombe
Gavin
Genet Moyle
George Carpenter
George Cave
George Neal
Gibbon's Russet
Gibby's Apple
Gilliflower of Gloucester
Gin
Gipsy King
Gladstone
Glasbury
Glass Apple
Glebe Gold
Gloria Mundi
Glory of England
Glory of the West
Gloucester Cross
Gloucester Royal
Golden Bittersweet
Golden Bounty
Golden Delicious
Golden Farmer
Golden Glow
Golden Harvey
Golden Knob
Golden Monday
Golden Noble
Golden Nonpareil
Golden Nugget
Golden Pearmain
Golden Pippin
Golden Reinette
Golden Royal
Golden Russet
Golden Spire
Golden Wonder
Goldilocks
Gold Medal

Gold Spur
Goodwood Pippin
Gooseberry
Goosberry Pippin
Goring
Grand Sultan
Grange's Pearmain
Granny Giffard
Granny Smith
Grantonian
Gravenstein
Greasy Pippin
Great Expectations
Green Balsam
Green Chisel
Green Custard
Green Harvey
Green Kilpandy Pippin
Green Pearmain
Green Purnell
Green Roland
Greensleeves
Greenup's Pippin
Grenadier
Grey Pippin
Grimoldby Golden
Guelph
Gulval Seedling
Haggerstone Pippin
Hagloe Pippin
Halstow Natural
Halton Barton
Hambledon Deux Ans
Hambling's Seedling
Hampshire Beauty
Hangy Down
Hannan Seedling
Hanwell Souring
Hapsburg
Harling Hero
Harlow Pippin
Harry Masters Jersey
Harry Pring
Harvest Festival
Harvest Peach
Harvey
Haughty's Red
Hawkridge
Hawthornden
Haye Farm
Hazen
Hebburn Red
Hector Macdonald

Henry Clay
Henry Davis
Henry Winch
Herbert Eastoe
Hereford Cross
Hereford Redstreak
Herefordshire Beefing
Herefordshire Pomeroy
Herman's Pippin
Herring's Pippin
Heusgen's Golden Reinette
Hibb's Seedling
Hibernal
High View Pippin
Histon Cropper
Histon Favourite
Hitchin Pippin
Hoary Morning
Hodge's Seedling
Hocking's Green
Hocking's Yellow
Hodge's Seedling
Hodkinson
Hog's Snout
Hollandbury
Holland Pippin
Hollow Core
Holly
Holstein
Honey Ball
Honey Pippin
Honeystring
Hood's Supreme
Hope Cottage Seedling
Hormead Pearmain
Horneburger Pfannkuchen
Horsford Prolific
Horsham Russet
Houblon
Hounslow Wonder
Howgate Wonder
Hubbard's Pearmain
Hunter Spartan
Hunter's Majestic
Hunt House
Huntingdon Codlin
Hunt's Deux Ans
Hunt's Duke of Gloucester
Hunt's Early Hunter
Hutton Square
Improved Cockpit
Improved Dove
Improved Hangdown

Improved Keswick
Improved Kingston Black
Improved Lambrook Pippin
Improved Redstreak
Improved Woodbine
Ingall's Pippin
Ingall's Red
Invincible
Irish Peach
Iron Pin
Isaac Newton's Tree
Isle of Wight Pippin
James Grieve
James Lawson
James Sanders
Jennifer
Jennifer Wastie
Jersey Beauty
Jester
John Apple
John Broad
John Divers
John Downie
John Huggett
Johnny Andrews
Johnny Voun
John Standish
John Waterer
Jolly Miller
Jonagold
Jonagored
Jonathan
Jordan
Jordan's Weeping
Joybells
Joyce Allardice
June Crewdson
Jupiter
Katy
Keed's Cottage
Keegan's Crab
Kemp
Kenneth
Kent
Kentish Fillbasket
Kentish Quarrenden
Kerry Pippin
Keswick Codlin
Kidd's Orange Red
Kilkenny Pearmain
King Albert
King Byerd
King Charles Pearmain

King Coffee
King Cox
King George V
King of the Pippins
King of Tompkins County
King Russet
King's Acre Bountiful
King's Acre Pippin
King's Favourite
Kingston Black
Knobby Russet
Lady Henniker
Lady Hollendale
Lady Hopetown
Lady Isabel
Lady of the Lake
Lady of the Wemyss
Lady Richardson
Lady Sudeley
Lady's Delight
Lady's Finger
Lady's Finger of Hereford
Lady's Finger of Lancaster
Lady's Finger of Offaly
Lady Thornycroft
Lake's Kernel
Lamb Abbey Pearmain
Lambrook Pippin
Lambrook Seedling
Lamb's Seedling
Lancashire Pippin
Lancashire Scotch Bridget
Landon
Lane's Oakland Seedling
Lane's Prince Albert
Lange's Perfection
Langley Pippin
Langworthy
Lass O'Gowrie
Lawry's Cornish Giant
Laxton's Early Crimson
Laxton's Favourite
Laxton's Fortune
Laxton's Herald
Laxton's Imperial
Laxton's Leader
Laxton's Pearmain
Laxton's Peerless
Laxton's Premier
Laxton's Rearguard
Laxton's Reward
Laxton's Royalty
Laxton's Superb

Laxton's Triumph
Laxton's Victory
Leatherjacket
Leathercoat Russet
Le Bret
Legana
Lemoen
Lemon
Lemon Pippin
Lemon Queen
Lemon Square
Lent Rise
Leonard Lush
Lewis's Incomparable
Liddel's Seedling
Lily Boxall
Limberland
Limelight
Listener
Livermere Favourite
Livsey's Codlin
Lobo
Lock Apple
Lockley's Nonsuch
Loddington
Lodgemore Nonpareil
Lodi
London Pearmain
London Pippin
Longbider
Longkeeper
Longney Russet
Long Reinette
Longstart
Long Stem
Long Tom
Lord Beatty
Lord Burghley
Lord Clyde
Lord Derby
Lord Derby Spur Type
Lord Grosvenor
Lord Hindlip
Lord Kelvin
Lord Kitchener
Lord Lambourne
Lord Lennox
Lord Nelson
Lord of the Isles
Lord Peckover
Lord Raglan
Lord Roberts
Lord Rosebery

Lord Stradbroke
Lord Suffield
Lorna Doone
Lucombe's Pine
Lucombe's Seedling
Lynn's Pippin
Mabbott's Pearmain
Maclean's Favourite
Madresfield Court
Magdalene
Maggie Grieve
Maggie Sinclair
Maid of Kent
Maiden's Blush
Maidstone Favourite
Major
Malcolm's Delight
Maldon Wonder
Maltster
Malus floribunda
Manaccan Promise
Manks Codlin
Mannington's Pearmain
Mareda
Margaret
Margaret Taylor
Margil
Marriage-Maker
Marston Scarlet
Martin's Kernel
Martin's Seedling
Mary Barnett
Mary Green
Mary's Apple
Matthew's Seedling
Maundy
Maxton
May Beauty
May Queen
Mead's Broading
Mealy Late Blossom
Measday Favourite
Melcombe Russet
Melmoth
Melrose
Merchant Apple
Mère de Ménage
Meridian
Merrigold
Merton Beauty
Merton Charm
Merton Delight
Merton Joy

Merton Knave
Merton Pearmain
Merton Pippin
Merton Prolific
Merton Reinette
Merton Russet
Merton Worcester
Michaelmas Red
Michaelmas Stubbard
Michelin
Middle Green
Miller's Seedling
Millet
Millicent Barnes
Minchall's Crab
Mitchelson's Seedling
Mollyanne
Monarch
Monkland Pippin
Monk's Golden Pippin
Monmouthshire Beauty
Morley's Seedling
Montfort
Morgan Sweet
Morning Pippin
Morris's Russet
Moss's Seedling
Mosses Seedling
Mother
Mountenay's Seedling
Mount Rainier
Mr Prothero
Mrs Barron
Mrs Lakeman's Seedling
Mrs Phillimore
Mrs Toogood
Mrs Wilmot
Munster Tulip
Murfitt's Seedling
Must
Nailsea White
Nancy Jackson
Nanny
Neild's Drooper
Nelson's Favourite
Nettlestone Pippin
Neverblight
New Bess Pool
New German
New Hawthornden
New Jonagold
New Northern Greening
New Rock Pippin

Newport Cross
Newton Wonder
Newtown Pippin
Nine Square
Nolan Pippin
Nonpareil
Nonsuch Park
No Pip
Norfolk Beauty
Norfolk Beefing
Norfolk Coleman
Norfolk Royal
Norfolk Royal Russet
Norfolk Summer Broadend
Northern Greening
Northland Seedling
Northwood
Norton Bitters
Nottingham Pippin
Nursery Asses
Nutmeg Pippin
Oaken Pin
Old English Pippin
Old Foxwhelp
Old Fred
Old Golden Russet
Old Middlemas
Old Pearmain
Old Somerset Russet
Onion Moonstreak
Ontario
Opal
Orange Goff
Orange Pippin
Orléans Reinette
Osier
Oslin
Owen Thomas
Oxford Beauty
Oxford Conquest
Oxford Hoard
Oxford Sunrise
Oxford Yeoman
Paignton Marigold
Palmer's Rosey
Parker's Pippin
Paroquet
Patrick
Payhembury
Peacemaker
Peachy Apple
Pear Apple
Pearl

Peasgood's Nonsuch
Pêche Melba
Peggy's Pride
Pendragon
Pennard Bitter
Penny Loaf
Perthyre
Peter Lock
Peter's Pippin
Peter's Seedling
Petworth Nonpareil
Pheasant's Eye
Philadelphia
Pickering's Seedling
Pig's Nose (111 JE)
Pig's Nose Pippin
Pig's Snout
Pine Apple Russet of Devon
Pine Golden Pippin
Pink Lady
Pinner Seedling
Pioneer
Pitmaston Pineapple
Pitmaston Russet Nonpareil
Pixie
Plum Vite
Plymouth Cross
Plympton King
Plympton Pippin
Polka
Polly
Polly Prosser
Polly Whitehair
Pomeroy
Ponsford
Poor Man's Profit
Port Allen Russet
Porter's Perfection
Pott's Seedling
Powell's Russet
Price's Seedling
Prince Alfred
Prince Charles
Prince Edward
Prince George
Prince's Pippin
Princess
Proctor's Seedling
Profit
Puckrupp Pippin
Puffin
Pyleigh
Pyne's Pearmain

Queen
Queen Alexandra
Queen Caroline
Queen Cox
Queen Cox (Maclean)
Queenie
Queenby's Glory
Queens
Quench
Quince
Radcliffe Nonpareil
Radford Beauty
Rakemaker
Rank Thorn
Rathe Ripe
Ravelston Pippin
Red Army
Red Blenheim
Red Charles Ross
Red Devil
Red Ellison
Red Falstaff
Red Foxwhelp
Red Glow
Redhill Sops in Wine
Red Jersey
Red Miller
Red Musk
Red Newton Wonder
Red Ribbed Greening
Red Robin
Red Rollo
Red Sauce
Red Sentinel
Redsleeves
Redstart
Redstrake
Redstreak
Red Sudeley
Red Victoria
Redwing
Red Windsor
Red Worthy
Reid's Seedling
Reinette de Champagne
Reinette de Versailles
Reinette du Canada
Reinette Rouge Etoilée
Renown
Reverend Greeves
Reverend W. Wilks
Reynold's Peach
Ribston Pippin

Richardson (Ashworth)
Richardson (Tomalin)
Rich's Favourite
Ringer
Rival
Rivers' Early Peach
Riversii
Rivers' Nonsuch
Robert Blachford
Robin Pippin
Rock
Rome Beauty
Ronald's Gooseberry
Rosa du Perch
Rosamund
Rosebery
Rosemary Russet
Rossie Pippin
Ross Nonpareil
Rosy Blenheim
Rougemont
Rough Pippin
Round White Nonesuch
Roundway Magnum Bonum
Roxbury Russet (Boston Russet)
Royal Gala
Royal George
Royal Jersey
Royal Jubilee
Royal Late Cooking
Royal Red
Royal Seedling
Royal Snow
Royal Somerset
Rubinette
Ruby (Seabrook)
Ruby (Thorrington)
Rymer
Saint Ailred
Saint Albans Pippin
Saint Augustine's Orange
Saint Cecilia
Saint Edmund's Pippin
Saint Everard
Saint Magdalen
Saint Martin's (Blackman)
Saint Martin's (Rivers)
Saltcote Pippin
Sam's Crab
Sam Young
Sandew
Sandlin Duchess

Sandringham
Sanford Jersey
Sanspareil
Saturn
Sawpit
Scarlet
Scarlet Crofton
Scarlet Nonpareil
Scarlet Pearmain
Schoolmaster
Scilly Pearl
Scotch Bridget
Scotch Dumpling
Scrumptious
Seabrook's Red
Seaton House
September Beauty
September Scarlet
Sercombes Natural
Sergeant Peggy
Severn Bank
Shakespeare
Sharleston Pippin
Sharpshooter
Shaw's Pippin
Sheep's Nose
Shepherd's Newington
Shinfield Seedling
Shoesmith
Shoreditch White
Sidney Strake
Silver Cup
Sir Douglas Haig
Sir John Thornycroft
Sisson's Worksop Newtown
Slack Ma Girdle
Sleeping Beauty
Small's Admirable
Smart's Prince Arthur
Smiler
Smiling Morn
Somerset
Somerset Lasting
Somerset Redstreak
Sops in Wine
South Park
Sovereign
Sowman's Seedling
Spartan
Spencer
Spencer Seedless
Springrove Codlin
Stable Jersey

Stamford Pippin
Stanway Seedling
Stark
Stark's Earliest
Star of Devon
Starkspur Golden Delicious
Stembridge Clusters
Stembridge Jersey
Stevenson Wealthy
Steyne Seedling
Stibbert
Stirling Castle
Stobo Castle
Stockbearer
Stocker's Seedling
Stoke Allow
Stoke Edith Pippin
Stoke Red
Storey's Seedling
Stradbroke
Strawberry Norman
Strawberry Pippin
Striped Beefing
Striped Brandy
Striped Early Cox Sport
Striped Sax
Striped Wellington
Strippy
Stubbard
Sturmer Pippin
S. T. Wright
Summer Apple
Summer Blenheim
Summer Golden Pippin
Summer John
Sunburn
Sundale
Sunnydale
Sunrise
Sunset
Sunset Sport
Suntan
Sure Crop
Surprise
Sussex Mother
Sweet Alford
Sweet Bay
Sweet Cleave
Sweet Coppin
Sweet Lading
Sweet Larks
Sweet Merlin
Sweet Orange

Sweet Pethyre
Sykehouse Russet
Symes
Tale Sweet
Tan Harvey
Taunton Cross
Taunton Golden Pippin
Taylor's
Taylor's Sweet
Teesdale Nonpareil
Ten Commandments
Tewkesbury Baron
Thoday's Quarrenden
Thomas Jeffrey
Thomas Rivers
Thompson's Apple
Thorle Pippin
Thorpe's Peach
Tiffin
Tillington Court
Tim's Early
Tinsley Quince
Tommy
Tommy Knight
Tommy Rodford
Tom Potter
Tom Putt
Topred
Topsy
Tower of Glamis
Town Farm
Transparente de Croncels
Tregonna King
Tremlett's Bitter
Trenance Cooker
Tun Apple
Tupstones
Twinings Pippin
Tydeman's Early
Tydeman's Late Orange
Tydeman's Michaelmas Red
Tyler's Kernel
Tyneham Apple
Uland
Underleaf
Upton Pyne
Valentine
Vallis
Veitch's Perfection
Veitch's Scarlet
Venus Pippin
Vicar of Beighton
Vickey's Delight

153

Victory (Carpenter)
Vilberie
Violette
Vista Bella
Voyager
Wadey's Seedling
Wadhurst Pippin
Wagener
Waltham Abbey Seedling
Waltz
Wanstall Pippin
Wappreham Russet
Warden
Wardington Seedling
Warner's King
Warren's Seedling
Wayside
Wax Apple
Wealthy
Wear and Tear
Webb's Russet
Weight
Welford Park Nonsuch
Welsh Russet
Weston's Seedling
West View Seedling
Wheeler's Russet
White Close Pippin
White Jersey

White Joaneting
White Melrose
White Norman
White Paradise
White Quarrenden
White Quaranatine
White Russet
Whitesour
White Transparent
White Winter Pearmain
Whiting Pippin
Wickham Green
Widow's Friend
William Crump
William Ingall
William Peters
Wilson's Endeavour
Wilton's Red Jonaprince
Winston
Winston Sport
Winter Banana
Winter Broadend
Winter Codlin
Winter Gem
Winter Gold
Winter Hawthornden
Winter Marigold
Winter Majetin
Winter Peach

Winter Pearmain
Winter Quarrenden
Winter Queening
Winter Stubbard
Wisley Crab
Withington Fillbasket
Withington Welter
Woodbine
Woodford
Woodstock Pippin
Woolaton Pippin
Woolbrook Pippin
Woolbrook Russet
Worcester Cross
Worcester Pearmain
Wormsley Pippin
Wyken Pippin
Yarlington Mill
Yellow Ingestrie
Yellow Pitcher
Yellow Redstreak
Yellowspur
Yellow Styre
Ye Old Peasgood
Yeovil Sour
Yorkshire Aromatic
Yorkshire Greening
Young's Pinello

T HIS CHAPTER GIVES ADVICE on the choice of trees, rootstocks, tree forms and size and explains the importance of matching pollination types. The field guide shows at least two types of apple per double page spread. Out of over 6,000 named apples, over 2,000 of which are in the national collection at Brogdale, Faversham, Kent, how have the 130 cultivars been selected? The guide cannot include every type found in orchards and gardens, but the selection here covers most of those brought for identification at Apple Days or in the major collections.

The Frank P. Matthews Nursery of Berrington Court, Tenbury Wells, Worcestershire, have kindly added their best selling newer types and these are included in the Field Guide as 'Growing in popularity' amongst the list that is broadly based on the great fruit expert Harry Baker's experience. I have added a number of others, but the guide represents about two hundred years of selection for high quality flavour and characteristics such as disease resistance and regular cropping. Every locality also has its own varieties (see pp.140-146) which can still be found, often in old gardens; there may be relic trees from orchards built over. Our heritage of fruit should be preserved and revived wherever possible. I would encourage readers to make their own list from their area. You can try out the different types at Apple Days organised locally or from Brogdale's apple tasting days for members and visitors, organised through the season. Do not turn up in late October and expect to taste an August variety, however, because these will have either all been sold or will not have kept that long.

The same points apply for garden apple tree planting as for flowers in your garden: choose a variety that thrives, not simply survives in your conditions. The more ornamental blossoms are a bonus and surprisingly well scented in some cases. I have found our wilding (tree of unknown name or origin) crab apples the strongest and longest lasting of all the blossoms. Whether they came from the out-grown rootstocks of our 70-year-old apple cordons or from self-sown pips, I cannot be sure. They were referred to as 'pollinators' by the original owner of the orchard, Molly Hopkyns, and certainly give a good source of pollen to the mighty Bramleys and younger trees nearby.

If you are likely to juice your fruit or make cider from your apples, add larger numbers of the good juice producers like Bramley's Seedling, Jonagold and Tom Putt to blend. There is an attractive colour sport of Jonagold with a play on the original name, called Jonagored (pronounced Jon-a-go-red). If the production of cider is your main objective it would be essential to read up on the subject and seek out good cider apple varieties. (See Copas, Deal and Williams in the Bibliography and visit demonstrations at places like Brogdale or farms in the West County that still make farmhouse ciders). I have been pleased to find that our modern juicer that separates the juice so effectively still leaves a residue of skin to start the cider making off. This means that the natural yeast in the apple skin that has survived the process gets to work as usual. We start the cider off on the tiles of a room with under-floor heating and it is usually possible to enjoy home-made cider in about six weeks.

If you are planning an orchard with a view to selling dessert apples (co-operative crop collection is ideal for a group of small orchards in a district), and Cox's Orange Pippin grows well on your soil, add, say, 10 Cox so as to meet future demand, but remember that newer types like Discovery, Katy and Jonagold will sell well and be ready to eat from a much earlier date. (If you are uncertain about what grows well locally, ask around and visit local horticultural shows where fruit growing experts exhibit their produce. They are usually very helpful with advice and if you can speak to the fruit and vegetable judges after their work is done on the day, so much the better). I like James Grieve, Jupiter, Laxton's Superb and Worcester Pearmain too. Russets are a special delight if properly ripened: Orleans Reinette and St Edmund's Pippin are favourites of mine.

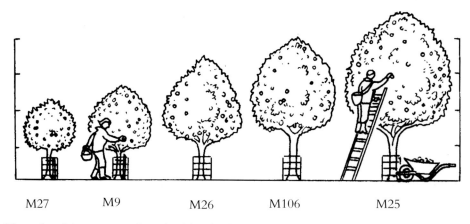

M27   M9   M26   M106   M25

I have plotted 1m steps on either side of this sketch of how different 10-12 year-old rootstocks will compare. Growth will also vary with soil quality and summer moisture.

Which rootstock?

The same types of apples grow on different sizes of rootstock. We would not consider for one moment going shopping for clothes without bothering to check what size they were or whether they will fit, yet   many people buy fruit trees at a garden centre without checking if the tree will grow to the size appropriate to the space they have available. A rule of thumb is that a tree will occupy the same space as its height, so that a fully grown standard apple of, say, 5 metres will take up a diameter of 5 metres of space around it, too. Apples do not grow true from their pips: instead they are bud or branch grafted onto a rootstock, the choice of which will affect the size of the final tree, the amount of fruit borne on the tree and also the speed with which it matures. This list gives the main rootstocks and their eventual heights:

M27	**1.5m (5-6')**	**Extremely dwarf**	Not on sandy soil. Can be used in pot cultivation. c20–30yrs life
M9	**1.8-3m (6-10')**	**Very dwarf**	No ground cover competition. c30–40yrs life suitable for cordons
M26	**2.4-3.6m (8-12')**	**Dwarf**	Not on heavy clay. Cordons.
MM106	**3.6-5m (12-18')**	**Semi-dwarf**	Suitable for all soils
M25	**5-6m (16-19')**	**Half standard/ Standard**	Suitable on all soils
MM111 and M2	**5-6.7m (18-22')**	**Vigorous**	Suitable on all soils

The rootstock numbers (M for Malling or MM for Merton–Malling) were given during the original field trials and do not indicate size.

The big fruit tree nurseries have catalogues which help in choice of rootstocks and descriptive publications from Bernwode Plants and Deacon's, for example, have advice on the rootstock size. They will supply you with multiples of, say, M106 or M25, according to your needs. I am all for the use of M25 (though it is not as widely available) because it makes an attractive and productive tree, although you have to wait longer for regular fruits, especially on the shy-cropping types. The best flavour will come from an apple picked from a tree at the right time.

M2 is deeper rooting than M9 and used in some commercial orchards. East Malling and Long Ashton Research Stations have also developed virus-free and woolly–aphid resistant rootstocks including EMLA7 that is ideal for planting amongst old trees at long established orchard sites.

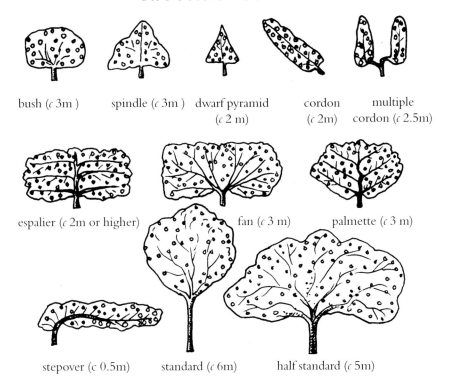

bush (*c* 3m)   spindle (*c* 3m)   dwarf pyramid (*c* 2 m)   cordon (*c* 2m)   multiple cordon (*c* 2.5m)

espalier (*c* 2m or higher)   fan (*c* 3 m)   palmette (*c* 3 m)

stepover (c 0.5m)   standard (*c* 6m)   half standard (*c* 5m)

Types of apple tree and their basic shapes when mature, about 10-12 years, with heights in brackets. In the multiple cordon: apples produce well in this form, and can also be grown in double 'U' shapes. They should not be trained in 3s, however, because the centre stem tends to dominate and leave 2 stragglers either side.

There are other rootstock types listed in Crawford and a helpful table of their effects on the growth of the tree and tolerance of conditions.

The first three (M27, M9 and M26) are for small spaces or large scale production in bush rows. The larger types, up to the full standard of MM111, will produce attractive individual trees for single spaces or small groups in gardens and community orchards intended to be a productive amenity and contribute to wildlife conservation for many years to come.

I do wish that nurseries would point out that one of the most widely sold semi-dwarfing rootstocks, M26, does not thrive on heavy clay soils. The dwarfed trees need stakes all through their rather short lives, hate competition from grass and need top quality soil, but they do come into production quicker and are easier to pick than the taller trees. Very heavy apples like Howgate Wonder will also put a considerable strain on their restricted branches.

What age?

You can plant a tree from one to three years old, but after that the tree will not transplant well. A one year old tree is called a 'maiden' and, if it has laterals, it is known as a 'feathered maiden'. This is preferable to the single stem maidens of one year, although these are cheaper. As long as the roots look in good order, pot grown trees will do well, but if you are ordering a large number of unusual types, an advance order from a catalogue will give the specialist nursery time to lift your trees at the best time of year. Be patient. If it has been too wet to lift them at the nursery, the same may be said of the ground where you are going to plant them. In any case, you should avoid ground that becomes waterlogged because apple trees do not survive well in these conditions. If you have a field that is more marshy at one end, or has a dip in the middle, keep this area for plums (and a perhaps a pond for wildlife).

It is best to buy your stock from a specialist nursery, although more and more garden centres offer a wide choice of apples. I wish more information was given guide to purchasers at garden centres about rootstocks and how suitable they may be. I think the time has probably come for a simple grade of tree types that the general public can follow easily.

If you are planting a new orchard you might well consider the bulk of the trees to be spindle bushes, but have a border of half standard and standard trees where they will be most visually attractive at the entrance or if seen from footpaths or roads. They help celebrate the presence of the orchard, where bushes might appear insignificant. These large trees should be grown on M25, M2 or MM 111 and become a feature of the site in later years. When the time comes, in about twenty to thirty years, to replace the dwarf trees, the standard apples will still have decades of productive life ahead of them as long as they are well cared for. Windfalls from trees that were too high to pick easily can be left for the winter thrush flocks. Windfall apples make an attractive feature of the autumn countryside.

The following apple tree types are spaced according to size as a general guide:

1 Standard or half standard	4–8m apart (13–30 feet)
2 Apple bush	3.5–5m (11–16 feet)apart or less
3 Apple spindle bush	2m (6 feet) apart or less
4 Dwarf pyramid	1–1.5m (3–4 feet) apart
5 Apple cordon	750mm apart in rows 2m (6 feet)
6 Multiple cordon	1.5m (4 feet) apart
7 Step-overs	1.5m (4 feet) apart
8 Apple espalier	4m (13 feet) or more apart
9 Apple fan	6m (19 feet)or more apart
10 Apple palmette	4m (13 feet) or more apart

Who pollinates whom?

Apple trees are not fully self-fertile and pollination is by insects that visit the trees when they are in blossom. Bees are so good at carrying pollen from tree to tree that beehives are often kept permanently in orchards. The trees are selected to grow in groups that come into flower at the same time so that pollination is at its most efficient even when cold, windy, wet weather may disrupt the insect activity for the duration of the blossom. All too quickly the petals blow away. Some blossom is more ornamental and attractive in the garden setting than others and the field guide refers to this in places. In choosing trees for an orchard you should, therefore, pick trees in the same flowering group as much as possible, or the group next in line. Flowering groups are given for each type in the guide, but on the opposite page you will also find the groups listed. Some apples, like Bramley's Seedling, are triploid and need two other trees in flower at the same time to pollinate them: thus three trees are involved in the production of their fruit. Most of the triploid trees I can think of are prolific, as long as the presence of other trees in the same pollination group are present. The groups indicate when the apple trees are in blossom, and all trees in the same group will cross-pollinate, because they are in flower at the same time, and also adjacent groups will pollinate because their timings will overlap. Catalogues from the best suppliers of apple trees will give the pollination group each variety belongs to so that you may make a selection which is likely to crop well. Some trees are partly self-fertile, but all do better if there are at least two in flower near each other at the same time. For the Bramley, it was popular to plant James Grieve, Grenadier and Cox to this end because all flower together. Cox's Orange Pippin defies the rules as it is cross-incompatible with Kidd's Orange Red and also with Holstein.

A crab apple such as John Downie or the presence of nameless wild crab apple trees in a nearby hedgerow can all help because they may stay in flower through the different flowerings of apples of various pollen groups. These nameless trees produce chance seeded apples of little value in terms of taste, sale or recognised quality, but can provide a basic juice for blending, wine or cider making and should not be ignored. They are a valuable source of food for wildlife and often stay late on the trees.

If, therefore, you are choosing apples to plant in an orchard, make your choice from the recommendations here, but remember not to neglect your local and unusual types because they will have a special appeal in flavour, looks and even historical connections to your site. This book is not, therefore, intended to encourage the reader to stick to just the popular varieties, wonderful fruit as they may be, but to get to know apples better, identify most that are found growing in Britain, seek out unusual types and ensure that the old varieties do not disappear for lack of knowledge about them. (For dessert and dual purpose, cooking, cider and crab distinguishing names, see the alphabetical lists from p.146).

Pollination table, starting with the earliest

T = Triploid (needs pollen of three trees)

B = Biennial or irregular in flowering

Group 1 Gravenstein (T), Stark's Earliest

Group 2 Adam's Pearmain (B), Alkmene, Beauty of Bath, Bismarck (B), Braeburn, Devonshire Quarrenden (B), Early Victoria, Egremont Russet, Elstar, George Cave, George Neal, Idared, Irish Peach, Keswick Codlin (B), Laxton's Early Crimson, Lord Lambourne, Margil, McIntosh Red, Merton Charm, Norfolk Beauty, Owen Thomas, Princess, Red Falstaff, Red Windsor, Rev. W. Wilks (B), Ribston Pippin (T), St Edmund's Pippin, Warner's King (T), Winter Gem

Group 3 Allington Pippin (B), Arthur Turner, Belle de Boskoop (T), Belle de Pontoise (B), Blenheim Orange (T)(B), Bountiful, Bramley's Seedling (T), Charles Ross, Cox's Orange Pippin, Crispin (T)(B), Discovery, Duchess's Favourite, Early Victoria(B), Emperor Alexander, Fiesta, Granny Smith, Greensleeves, Grenadier, Hambledon Deux Ans, Hitchin Pippin, Holstein (T), James Grieve, John Standish, Jonathan, Jupiter (T), Katy, Kent, Kidd's Orange Red, Lane's Prince Albert, Laxton's Epicure, Laxton's Fortune (B), Lord Grosvenor, Lord Hindlip, Malling Kent, Mère de Ménage, Merton Knave, Merton Worcester, Miller's Seedling (B,) Nonpareil, Peasgood Nonsuch, Queen, Red Delicious, Rival (B), Rosemary Russet, Scrumptious, Spartan, Stirling Castle, Sturmer Pippin, Sunset, Tom Putt, Tydeman's Early, Wagener (B), Wealthy, Worcester Pearmain

Group 4 Annie Elizabeth, Ashmead's Kernel, Autumn Pearmain, Barnack Beauty, Brownlees' Russet, Chiver's Delight, Claygate Pearmain, Cornish Aromatic, Cornish Gillyflower, Cox's Pomona, D'Arcy Spice, Duke of Devonshire, Dumelow's Seedling, Ellison's Orange, Encore, Gala, Gladstone (B), Golden Delicious, Golden Noble, Harvey, Herring's Pippin, Howgate Wonder, Jonagold (T), King's Acre Pippin, Lady Sudeley, Laxton's Superb (B), Lord Burghley, Lord Derby, Monarch (B), Orlean's Reinette, Pixie, Tower of Glamis, Tydeman's Late Orange, Winston

Group 5 Gascoyne's Scarlet (T), King of the Pippins (B), Lady Henniker, Merton Beauty, Mother, Newton Wonder (B), Nonpareil, Norfolk Royal, Royal Jubilee, Suntan (T), William Crump

Group 6 Bess Pool, Court Pendu Plat, Edward V11

Group 7 Crawley Beauty

The apple as food

The apple is one of those rare fruits that is not only very important for our health, but can be used with meat dishes as well as in desserts. A sweet apple can be eaten as a 'raw' dessert, usually quartered with cheese or on its own, or cooked.

It is so quick to cook apples and the flavour of a Bramley, baked with a sprinkle of raisins and brown sugar or stewed and eaten with ice cream, is superb. Blackberry and apple pie, when you have picked both ingredients and eaten them within hours, is a taste sensation we should be proud of. Our cooking traditions have been so sneered at through the last century, when shortages from conflicts often produced poor quality 'survival rations', that we seem to have lost the confidence to be proud of our great dishes.

Corer, peeler and slicer.

Having fruit in our diet is now known to be much better for us than fatty meats (much as I enjoy both), yet our agricultural policies favour meat production at the expense of what we do well - growing some of the best, most varied fruit in the world. What is more, we have nearly lost the expertise and knowledge which ensured the survival of a great variety of fruit production.

The choice in our shops is now often limited to very few types of apple, picked much too early and transported to this country from abroad. Some have been sprayed no less that eight times through the annual cycles of the trees involved. Yet you cannot beat the flavour of an organically grown dessert apple which is in season when you pick it ripe from a tree. The American variety, Golden Delicious, is superb when picked matured on its twigs and eaten fresh from an English garden fruit tree, yet many decry this variety because of imports of fruit picked 'raw' before the apple has ripened properly.

I always remember a guide as we toured Brogdale's orchards saying, 'It is only for those of us who have such a wonderful choice of apples to call an apple a "cooker" or an "eater". In most countries an apple is just an apple and is cooked or eaten fresh without the luxury of choice we have here.' We have done our best to lose that choice, even though we must have one of the best climates and types of soil for hardy fruit production in the world.

I found an old cutting in my 1973 diary: 'MAFF says that now is the time to grub up your unproductive orchards or you will lose the grants which cannot be paid after October.' This shows the pressure put on farmers and landowners to grub up their orchards. As we created grain mountains we lost our great orchard tradition, but it is not too late to recover this.

Apple wedger.

Breville juicer.

5 Planting

A S WELL AS BEING A GUIDE TO APPLE TYPES, THIS BOOK IS INTENDED TO HELP YOU if you are planning to plant an apple tree or have an orchard in mind. Using the descriptions in the field guide (Chapter 2), you can select the type of apples that will suit your circumstances best.

In the garden or patio a light location is essential. If you have a field site you might set out a grid for all the 130 types illustrated in the field guide section, with an additional 20 local, less known, types and blocks of 10 of the most popular varieties. The lists (p.140) will help in this choice. I do not, however, want to encourage the idea that orchards are just a luxury at sites where space is available. We can at last seriously consider orchards on a commercial basis once again as public interest has returned to appreciate the importance of fruit as an essential part of a healthy diet. The more local and national the production, the better for all concerned.

The first essential, whether you have a dwarfed tree in a pot, a standard apple tree in the middle of a lawn, a set of 40 trees in a small paddock or a vast orchard, is *light*. Apple trees will only thrive if strong daylight surrounds them through most of the day. The soil must be deep and well drained and shelter is important, too. In the descriptions I have included those, like Gascoyne's Scarlet, that cope with chalk soil, but it is worth checking that your planting site is not over a hidden brick foundation to some long lost building or road, especially if you are planting half-standard on M25 rootstock, or taller trees, which will send down deep roots. Ground drainage is also affected by such hidden barriers.

If a screen from the prevailing wind does not exist at an open site, grow a shelter belt set back from the trees so as not to shade them. Avoid dense blocks of trees because wind then dips over the top and causes turbulence rather than calm on the other side. A quickly formed, less dense, barrier of native trees and shrubs including such types as blackthorn, rowan and wild service will be of benefit to wildlife. This will grow as the fruit trees mature. It is best to avoid hawthorn because it is the host plant for the *Fireblight* bacteria, although I must admit our orchard is surrounded by hawthorn and it is a rich source of food to the birds and insects we rely on to do our control of harmful species. We get excellent crops from Conference and Fertility pears. We propagate and plant wild service trees along with the apple trees because they are also a very attractive and fruitful source of food for wildlife, but the official line is that they should not be planted because they are used to date old hedgerows. I can think of no better way of condemning a beautiful tree to oblivion than this sort of 'hedgerow planting rule'.

Whether you propagate your own trees, order them from a nursery, or buy them 'off the shelf' in a garden centre, the way you plant them is important.

We have already discussed the selection of types to ensure that your tree or trees thrive, not just survive. Problems in the future life of the tree can date right back to how it was planted and its condition then. One of the common faults is to purchase a pot-bound tree that is being sold off cheaply because the roots are emerging from the drainage holes underneath. I have heard one broadcaster dispute that the existence of prolonged, curled, stunted roots should cause the tree to become unstable and fail to thrive. It is said that you just pull out the roots evenly round the tree and this tendency will disappear. However, many people do not notice the root condition and some curl is so long set that you cannot rectify the curve. Even if you try to spread the distorted roots in a young tree they can retain the tendency, but careful loosening of the root ball is always a help as you sink it into a light compost soil mix in the hole.

My drawing (overleaf) illustrates a 'bargain' Cox's Orange Pippin that never thrived and kept tilting. The roots proved to be badly distorted and the few pounds saved meant years of wasted attention and loss of useful space. Some specialist nurseries prefer to sell their trees in pots because they feel bare roots get damaged when they are lifted and time is lost as they make up ground. This is fine if the trees have not been in the pot too long, they are not planted in very dry conditions and they are watered regularly until well established.

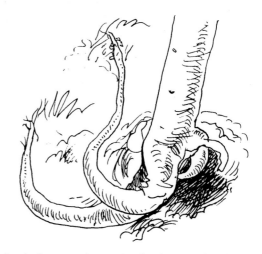

We have done well with both forms, but I am still very wary of pot-bound specimens. A 17 year old Monarch I moved to a light location from a shaded garden where it had never produced an apple had curled roots like propeller blades from pot restriction, but it has since done well in our orchard with other Monarchs nearby and started cropping in its second year. So the damage does last and become a permanent feature, but can be compensated for by a strong stake, a light, open location and new root growth to tether the tree well in the ground.

Avoid frost hollows, unless this is the only space you have. In that case, select the very late flowering apple varieties that can produce well in these sites. (I have made a note of these in the descriptions in chapter 2, from p.14. Edward V11, Encore, Wagener and Winston are good examples).

At night frost will roll down a hill through an orchard planted on a slope and collect in the lowest point. Modern freezing techniques where the trees are sprayed to form a thick protective ice coat in northern climes and the use of burners to prevent frost are two of the more extreme techniques used by some growers. Typical damage to the blossom comes as the sun rises and burns through the ice: it has a magnifying effect and the young apples do not set. Really severe, chill downpours can also damage the fruit as it is setting, especially if hailstones are involved. The delicate little applets are simply knocked off by the force of the rain or ice droplets.

With prevailing west wind conditions, protection from the wind on one side and a similar screen to help the trees warm up before the sun reaches over the top on the other will help. I must repeat that light is the vital ingredient for fruit trees and if it is combined with protection from the worst of the elements, so much the better.

Although older trees (over 2 years) are harder to establish, ask if any are available if you have a garden site where you can water regularly and ensure that they are well fertilized and mulched as they adapt to their new location. The more unusual types of apple often remain unsold for longer than the popular ones and you can gain a year or two on production with older trees as long as they are carefully lifted and deeply planted. You can also fit wire mesh guards on taller trees to protect them against rabbits, sheep or deer without the risk of these mammals reaching over the top to eat the leaves and stems of the smaller trees.

Some nurseries will also propagate to order if you give them enough time. A selection of contacts is given on p.174 and catalogues can be ordered over the internet now. On arrival, heel the trees in at once unless they are pot grown or you can plant them straight away. Never allow bare roots to dry out, but it is not ideal to soak them with water unless they have somehow become seriously dehydrated because this will wash off any damp soil clinging to them. November still has fairly warm soil which is usually wet and if you plant between this month and mid-March, your bare-rooted trees will develop some root growth and settle in before they become really active in spring. Pot cultivated trees give more flexibility to planting times and suffer less of a shock in the move from nursery to final site, but need just as much after-care as bare-rooted ones.

The sap starts to rise in mild March conditions, and this is when the roots have to maintain the tree with ample moisture. If they have not been established long enough you can lose the trees if a prolonged drought follows. Even whilst you wheelbarrow young trees round during planting, windy conditions can dry out roots remarkably quickly and a wet sack over a light covering of compost will prevent this.

All trees should have a stake to mark out the layout of the holes to be dug and I like to use freshly cut ash posts about 1 or 2 m long, cut on a local nature reserve during routine management work. These should be set upside down to prevent them taking root themselves. If you are planting trees that need permanent stakes, then use posts treated with a wood preserver.

Site the tree on the side of the stake which is away from the prevailing wind and you will then provide the essential restraint with slight movement that a tree needs to grow strong root anchorage. Without the initial stake your tree will be unlikely to grow upright and be very vulnerable to falling over or even damage from animals leaning against the young trunk. It may also be blown about so much that a gap appears round the base from the movement and water logging develops at this point.

The lower down the tie is set on the tree the more natural movement the trunk is given, but make sure wire guards do not damage the bark they are protecting. I have seen so many forgotten tree ties and label cords cutting into trees that they make me nervous. It is so easy to overlook them and in the right conditions, fruit trees can expand very rapidly. Label twine quickly cuts into the bark if not removed. Although it is important to know the name of the tree, it is best to remove the label and drop it into the bottom of the wire shelter for future reference. Ideally, tie it to the wire mesh inside the guard.

You should keep an orchard plan of layout and names before you lose the labels and keep a copy of these with the deeds of the property if possible. Even a single garden tree should be named with the legal papers connected with the ownership of the house. It will help preserve the tree as well as record its name if you treat it with the respect such a garden feature deserves. Future owners might also be less inclined to chop it down.

Tree protectors should be fitted immediately and always be open wire mesh, wide enough to allow free growth without wear on lower branches. Tree tubes widely used on trees in plantations are airless and not suitable for fruit trees. You get problems of mildew, although this can be reduced by drilling the plastic with a power tool to create a scattering of holes. However, the airflow round the tree is not as good as that provided by fine, open wire mesh. Tubes accelerate growth in trees, but it is not worth the increased risk of disease with apples. They can be used as a temporary cover until the wire surrounds are fitted, but should not be a long term solution to protection.

Take a wheelbarrow with compost mixed with an organic granular fertilizer to aid root development and only dig the hole for your tree when you are ready to plant it inside. I used to mix in bone meal to accelerate root growth, but this is not recommended in organic cultivation now. (When I planted a Hitchin Pippin recently I buried a dead ferret below its roots, but this is not essential.)

It may seem a good idea to have all the holes dug in advance, but they may either become waterlogged or dry out too much. Put turf to one side and dig the hole wide and deep to accommodate all the roots. The posts can be knocked in with a hammer or post driver, but whatever method you use, make sure they set in really firmly. If livestock is going to share the field, really strong stakes and wire protectors are vital. They give stability as the tree establishes itself with upright growth. For a layout of M 25 rootstocks in one of our local Millennium Orchards we set out posts at 7m gaps in a grid across the field. We used a long architect's tape measure to keep the lines straight and set the second posts 3.5m in from the first to create as much space and light between trees. As a Community Orchard for visitors to walk amongst and picnic in, ample space was felt to be a priority, whilst a commercial orchard (aimed at maximum production) will have dwarfing rootstocks and closer set trees.

The holes for the trees should be wide and deep enough to take the roots without folding them at the tips and so that the graft point is well above the final soil surface level. A depth of

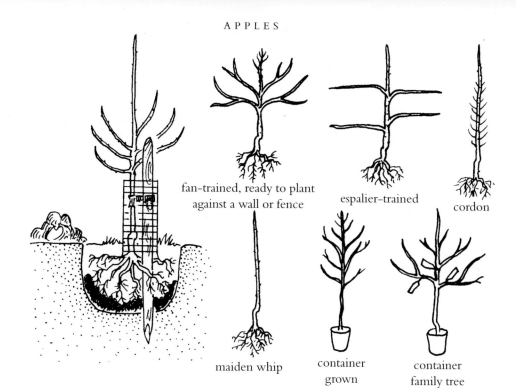

fan-trained, ready to plant
against a wall or fence

espalier-trained

cordon

maiden whip

container
grown

container
family tree

(Left to right) Planting an apple tree shown in cross section: dig a deep, wide hole in a light, well drained site that will take the roots without any restriction or crushing. The graft union near the base of the tree should stand clear of the ground level. A rich compost with granular fertilizer can be added at the bottom of the hole, but manure may be too strong and kill the tree. Drive a strong stake into place to ensure vertical growth of the tree. Make sure that the soil is trodden down firmly so that the roots are in contact with earth and not left with air pockets. Fit a wire protector and sink it below the back-filled soil. Water freely and fit a tie to the post and tree with plenty of space for growth. Check this regularly to avoid constriction and water the area, especially in dry spells. There is a wide choice of trees available, and some examples are illustrated. Bare-rooted trees are planted November to early March, whilst container grown trees can be planted at any time as long as they are kept watered.

350mm is usually adequate and you should make sure the roots are spread out evenly around the tree. Avoid filling the hole with strong, fresh manure that may well be so potent that it kills the tree. Old, light compost with granular fertilizer is ideal and will allow water easily to get to the young roots in the months and early years ahead as the tree establishes itself.

Gently shake the tree as you back fill the hole and make sure it sits well without trapped air gaps round the roots. A feathered maiden already has a pattern of branches and you should present the tree as you think it looks best in its setting. Tread the soil down firmly so that it is pressed against the roots and water the whole area thoroughly. In the garden you can regularly water, but out in a large orchard they will depend much more on rainfall and a bark mulch over the top of the bare soil will help retain moisture below ground level. It also helps to reduce grass growth which creates a barrier to water penetration into the soil.

Mulch mats allow water through whilst preventing grass growth, but can attract voles to nest underneath where it is more cosy than open pasture. These small mammals may delight in nibbling the tree bark and should be discouraged so close to the trunk. Protective paint is not yet legal in Britain, but has been shown to work well on bark for about two years in countries where it is used. Combined with wire mesh tree guards, it is probably the answer for tree protection against mammals in the future.

ECAUSE YOUNG TREES NEED ALL THEIR ENERGY to build up root and branch growth it is best to remove the first young apples that set for a year or two, however tempting it is to take your first small crop in the season ahead. This is less important in a fussed garden tree that has received constant watering and periodic gifts of granular fertilizer around the base. The shy cropping apple types may not treat you to fruit for some years anyway and that is a characteristic you should take into account. When a tree is well established it is helpful to thin the growing apples in order to get larger sized fruit. It also reduces the tendency to biennial cropping in many varieties. This can happen when a very vigorous tree produces extremely heavy crops of numerous small apples. The tree sheds a certain amount itself through the 'June drop', but you can add to this thinning process by taking the smallest, most crowded apples. If you reduce each group of five to two good specimens these will achieve the appropriate size for the type.

Pruning can take place at almost any time of year with apples, where appropriate, but only in spring or summer with plums for fear of disease like silver leaf entering the cut stems in cold, damp weather. Bare trees in winter show up the shape and needs of the apple tree best. Dead wood is particularly obvious and I inspect the tree for a short time before working clockwise round the trunk. The most obvious pruning to do is to remove dead or damaged branches. Unfortunately this type of wood blunts your loppers and secateurs more than living wood, but is a priority for removal. I have listed the tip-bearing and spur-bearing characteristics of different apples throughout Chapter 2 and you should bear this in mind as you open up the centre of a tree to let more light in. With spur-bearing trees, the idea of pruning is to shorten the laterals (side shoots) over successive years so that eventually they become spurs. With tip-bearers, the main aim of pruning is to open the tree out and cut out diseased or dead wood. The leaders (tallest, central stems) in general do not need to be pruned.

Whilst opening up the middle is the basic requirement, you can also prune to traditional shapes and forms, see illustration. Branches which cross over and rub others should be removed, and side shoots should be pruned to give short twigs on which the fruit forms in the case of spur-bearers, but if your tree is a tip-bearer and you keep cutting off the fruit-bearing wood from last year you will lose your apples. The spur-bearers which bear on two-year-old wood usually produce quicker and are easier to harvest than tip-bearers and can be more rigorously pruned. By thinning a tangle of branches and cutting back tight to outward facing buds to avoid die-back of short lengths of stems you will give daylight to the growing apples next season. On young trees it is common practice to take out the leader, so that the tree bushes out more. Several branches then compete to be leaders and you can regularly reduce those in the centre. Excessive pruning can, however, produce more vigorous branch growth without necessarily more fruit, just as drought in an old tree can set off the production of a mass of 'water shoots' (branches growing out from the main boughs or up the trunk). These are just a response to the stress of reduced water to the roots and can be cut off level with the main tree wood unless they occur at a section that needs renewal. There are many guides to pruning that often confuse the reader with complicated diagrams and endless references to what you should do to 'laterals' (side shoots) which are hard to follow. I strongly recommend the recent *RHS Pruning and Training Handbook* by Christopher Brickell and David Joyce because it is very clear and easy to follow. It shows the popular sizes and shapes of apple trees and the techniques for keeping them in shape for the best production of fruit. With our volunteer labour on the old trees at Tewin, restoration is a gentle matter and we seldom catch up with all the work set out in the management plan. We never attack the trees with major surgery that allows disease access. Old trees carry such a burden of bacteria and pests in their surroundings just waiting to

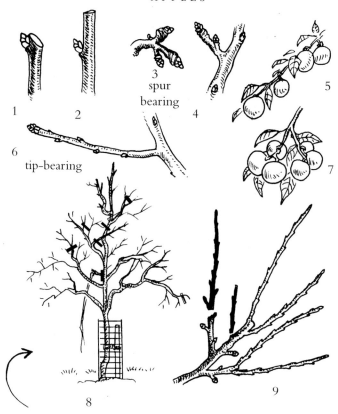

1
2
3
spur
bearing
4
5
6
tip-bearing
7
8
9

(Left to right, top) Pruning should always be carried out with clean, downward sloping cuts just above buds (1), rather than leaving a length of stem that will suffer die-back and may introduce infection into the tree (2). Spur-bearing trees develop buds in clusters rather like a cockerel's foot with spur (3). Do not prune a natural fruit spur at the branch tip (4), but in later years, you can thin out old, crowded spurs. Young apples grow along the branch from the spurs (5).
(Middle, left) A tip-bearing stem (6) that has a fruit bud on the end of a shoot and a typical cluster of tip-borne young apples (7). The object of the exercise in pruning is to get a succession of side branches growing each year of old growing shoots, two-year budding shoots and three-year-old fruiting shoots. Vigorous types such as the Bramley achieve this themselves without pruning, but even they benefit from thinning out old spurs and dead or damaged wood.
(8) shows my route approaching a tree to see what needs to be done. If you regularly work in a clockwise direction, you are less likely to miss branches in need of attention. Uprights and poorly developing stems (9) can be pruned back to a few buds or to the main branch.

get the upper hand that thinning and dead branch removal is all that is necessary. Some partly dead boughs that have living branches growing from them are left for the nest sites and insect food they provide the birds. I have seen so many examples of major trees that have had their limbs savaged and then died in subsequent drought years. One of the finest old beech trees in Epping Forest happened to shed a small section of dead wood where school parties visit and for 'health and safety' reasons was treated to the 'Venus de Milo' form of arm surgery only to die in the following few dry years which happened to follow. With the young trees we have planted amongst the old trees and elsewhere in the new orchard sites, the general advice is to reduce a vigorous young tree by about a quarter of the previous season's growth. This really helps the trees and makes them more productive.

I
F YOU HAVE SPACE TO PROPAGATE, so much the better, because it enables you to 'make your own' trees from cuttings (scions) of the unusual types which cannot easily be obtained from a nursery. Options for the propagation of apples are legion. My favourite guide to this is Robert Garner's *The Grafter's Handbook* which was first published in 1947 and is still in print. (The bookshop at the RHS Gardens, Wisley, usually has copies available.) He shows more ways to multiply fruit trees than you would ever need, but this encourages you to experiment.

Some friends look upon me grafting one branch to a stem as the work of some kind of failed, demented surgeon taking my frustration out on trees, but apples are open pollinated (fertilized from other apples) and do not grow the same variety from their pips. The pip that produced the 'one in a million' superb new type grown in the wild from a discarded core or deliberately grown in the hopes of a viable new type is the very rare exception. The cross-pollinations that produced the types in our illustrated field guide pages were the results of years of trials and experiments.

There are so many excellent varieties available that unless you want to spend your life in what might be a literally fruit-less pursuit of the 'ultimate apple', you are best advised to take cuttings from the known tried and tested trees of your choice, especially if they are rare ones which need attention if they are to survive for future generations to enjoy. To believe there is one, perfect, ultimate, apple out there waiting to be produced by cross pollination is like believing that there is only one really great painting or piece of music. The appreciation and cultivation of apples is as much an art as a botanical exercise as far as I am concerned.

That is also why I prefer to plant standard apple trees for the community to enjoy many years

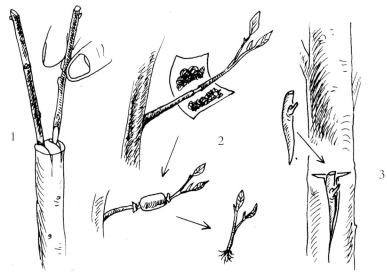

(Left to right) With older rootstocks I use 2 cleft grafts with the cuttings from, say, a James Grieve, cut to about 4 buds' length and sharpened to a wedge on both sides where they enter the cut rootstock (1). Air-layering (2) is useful in summer and the bark of a young shoot is ring-barked. Add hormone rooting powder and pack with damp compost. Seal the cut area within black polythene, tied at each end. Shield budding (3) with a T cut in the bark of a rootstock is another summer form of propagation. Tie in the bud from the tree with grafting tape so that it is secure inside the bark of the rootstock. Once the bud has established itself, and the protective tape has been removed, the rest of the rootstock growing above can be cut back to this new stem.

Chip budding: cut bud carefully from summer branch; remove all leaves (close-up shows the initial knife-cut below the bud and bud neatly being sliced). Next 3 stages are on the rootstock: a matching size of bark is cut off with a slight cleft at the base to grip the new bud. Bud is inserted and then wrapped with grafting tape to hold it firmly in place. When the union is completed, tape should be removed before it constricts the growing wood.

hence. There is a place for both: efficient, well-marketed commercial production and aesthetic tree planting for the future. You can plant margins of fruit trees that will grow tall and show colourful blossom as well as fruit around the lines of bush trees - even mix them like woodlands that have coppice and standards mingled. Your bushes will only crop well for about twenty years, but can be replaced as the standards go from strength to strength. I cannot think Samuel Palmer would have been inspired to paint the blossom and fruit on trees in his Shoreham period if he could only see lines of bushes around him.

In the case of the Hitchin Pippin I was able to take young branches from a youthful centre trunk in what is otherwise a very venerable centenarian tree. With the permission of the owners, Gerald and Elizabeth Rose, we divided the scions (cuttings of last year's twig growth) between the rootstocks at Tewin, Brogdale and Wisley so that the national collections would be able to include this type. The reason I tried to graft these at higher points on the rootstocks at home was because Gascoyne's Scarlet had taken really well in this way and, despite the long wait for initial signs of life, it paid off. The grafts were made on 9 March and the buds 'came alive' (as the graft union successfully transferred the sap to the alien scion) between two and three months later. You can usually tell if a graft is not going to take because the scion bark dries out and becomes ribbed.

I have found that the whip and tongue grafting illustrated here with Hitchin Pippin scions at different heights on the rootstocks has worked well, although the two month wait for the first buds to open, despite lots of leaf growth below, was unnerving. The tallest grafts took three months to come to life. The standard method of this type of grafting, for example, is low down, about 300mm above the soil surface, on a pencil-thin maiden rootstock. However, we have such problems with rabbit damage to young trees that the higher and older you can have your rootstocks, the better to get the trees away. It does mean you must remove all growth below your graft until the tree 'becomes the new type' you have chosen, or you will end up with a family tree of more than one type. These are often sold as a novelty and can be fun in garden pot cultivation, but there is a tendency for a more vigorous cultivar to dominate the other and the lop-sided or oddly mixed branch development can be unattractive.

Professionally grown dwarf bush trees often develop a rather tortured look, with swollen trunks just above the graft point and carefully trained, heavily pruned branches rather like battery hens in cages. This may seem absurd to say, but although the sprays and careful thinning of fruit to produce the smoothest skinned, large apples are very successful and productive, our trees, which are never sprayed and never heavily pruned, produce well and are so much more attractive to the eye. With air pollution, no tree can be really 'organic' but whilst I happily taste our fruit from the tree with a 'hygienic' wipe on a usually grubby pullover, I would hesitate to do the same with unwashed fruit on regularly sprayed trees. It is recommended to peel all shop-bought apples due to spraying and the automatic peeler we use is shown on p.160.

I expect the new techniques of micropropagation you now see in flower and shrub nurseries will be general for fruit trees one day, too. There may also be some form of type identification devised by chemistry one day. It is, however, very rewarding both to graft and chip-bud (see the illustration) your own trees. I was taught these methods by Duncan Cree in his orchard by the River Hiz at Ickleford, through the kind help of Jim Sutton, who farmed there. We started grafting plums on the wild stock that grew freely along the damp marsh and many of our present orchard trees were originally wild rootstocks from this site near Hitchin.

My grafting starts as the sap begins to rise in the trees during February and March. After that, chip budding can take place at almost any time in the following months and 'T' budding (see the drawing) is ideal as the growth of the young trees peak. Many years ago Chris Gooden at Brogdale demonstrated to me why I was failing with whip and tongue grafts on the thicker, older trees. This type of graft is suitable to pencil-thick stems that are not much wider than the scion wood. For older, thicker stems, cleft grafts and various types of shield budding techniques are best and I was very grateful for the advice of a master fruit grafter.

Taking the scion or cutting from the variety of tree you want to grow is not always easy in very old specimens. Their branches are usually growing high off the ground and the wood you can reach is often heavily spurred and encrusted with lichens. Seek out a young trunk and if necessary climb a ladder up to the young branches of last year's growth. Cut off enough to have a reasonable selection and if you are not grafting within a few days, shorten the scions into 500mm lengths, put them in a polythene bag and store them in the refrigerator. Do *not* put them in the frozen section or a deep freeze. Let them 'breathe': it is best not to tie up the top of the bag or you may find mildew develops. I have used scions kept this way for several months,

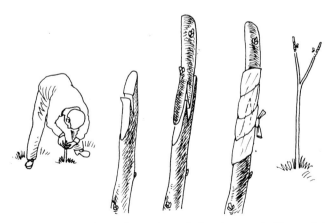

Whip-and-tongue grafting. Usually made near base of selected rootstock. Rootstock is cut to give an incision that will grip the graft wood. Cutting (scion) is cut to match the length of exposed wood, with a 'tongue' to fit into the rootstock. This is secured with grafting tape. Rootstock can be grafted at several points and higher up, but in this case any growth of branches below the new scions must be regularly cut off to ensure new tree is one type only.

but a few weeks is best, if you have to keep them at all. The great thing is to maintain them in moist, cold conditions so that the buds remain dormant.

A very important point about the scion is to only cut four bud lengths when you come to make your graft. It is tempting to think that you will get a longer, stronger branch with lots of buds, but the sap simply does not have the vigour to reach more than a few in the cutting. Even if it starts well, the stem is likely to wither and die back in the weeks that follow.

I rub off most of the young leaves appearing below the graft as early as possible because later a large, open twig wound is left. Do not be too efficient, however, in case the rootstock itself gives up the ghost as well. This treatment means that all the tree energy seeks out the buds and the ones on the graft thus receive maximum support.

The next opportunity I take is to chip-bud during the warm months (ideally from June to the end of August) and I have also had success with air-layering. This is where you cut the bark away from the surface of a thin, young branch to expose a length of its cambium layer (the soft, wet layer of cells between the bark and the wood). It is best to add some hormone rooting powder in the handful of damp compost you then press round it and tie this top and bottom inside black polythene. If carried out in June or July, you can usually find root growth at the exposed area as you gently examine the compost in September. The branch can then be cut away completely from the tree and potted up. This is particularly useful if you want to plant standard trees of known type because they will not then be on any form of rootstock and will grow freely. To see the vigour a Bramley, for example, is capable of, is a treat in itself.

When pips are planted they produce a tree which bears apples of whatever type of pollen was brought to the host tree. They do not, therefore, 'breed' true; propagation of the named varieties is either by grafting in the spring or chip budding in summer. If a tree has branches which grow down to the ground, which may happen if the tree has fallen over in a gale but continues to fruit and is left, you can layer the branches by pegging them down into the soil. This will produce a tall standard tree of that variety. Chance pips, however, and many rootstocks which have survived the original variety grafted or budded onto them, produce an assortment of generally small, wilding apples which are referred to as 'pollinators' or crab apples described earlier. They rarely taste like one of the popular dessert apples, but can be good for cider, juice and wine making, especially when blended with other varieties. They have produced some of the great apple types, but it will take thousands of trees of this kind to find a really exceptional one and it is best to stay with the varieties we have.

There was a plea by the Poultry Club to stop breeding any more varieties of chickens recently and much the same could probably be said by the national fruit collections: there are more than enough types to be getting on with! I have, however, enjoyed growing Red Devil, for example, cultivated by retired Brogdale fruit expert Hugh Ermen, and he continues to propagate new varieties, including the delicious Scrumptious (p.139) in Kent. New varieties may show valuable disease resistance and better flavour.

8 Pests and diseases

THE LIST OF DISEASES APPLE TREES can suffer from is likely to discourage you from ever planting one, just as the varieties of illness poultry get make you wonder how any chicken ever survives more than a week or two. In reality fruit trees from good stock prosper without much trouble as long as they are planted well and grown in light conditions.

Colourful guides are often produced to encourage you to spray your trees against all these threats. We never use sprays and whilst we are not following the traditional commercial methods, I am impressed with how well the trees cope with all the threats around them. Rabbit damage has been our most significant problem, both with young and old tree cultivation. The value in giving a young tree fertilizer and compost around the roots is to give the young tree as vigorous a start in life as possible. I also sprinkle sulphate of potash in the soil around the trees. A light situation and continuous care with water and attention to such features as ties and protection should result in a strong tree that resists disease without the need for sprays.

Use of the EMLA rootstocks helps with this vital, natural disease resistance, but you should do all you can to reduce any source of stress to the tree. I have experienced problems with canker where the trees have been planted in unfavourable locations amongst old trees, but although the advice is to cut the damaged wood out immediately and burn it to prevent it being spread to other trees, where this has been in a main stem and would have virtually meant cutting the tree down, the tree has recovered and repaired the canker site itself. This is obviously likely to be a future weakness where it could snap off in a gale, but with so much disease endemic around an old orchard it is not possible to remove it from such an area anyway. I am hopeful that such trees will continue to show good growth and survive. If you have ever snapped off a branch at a cankered joint you will know how vulnerable it makes a tree, but orchards where sprays are used all the time result in a loss of resistance to diseases.

If spraying ceases, apple trees may take several years to recover a robust immune system, but they will usually be back to normal production in five years. Modern shop sales demand blemish-free apples and the spray regime is in response to this. We select the perfect-looking apples and reject those that look marked in any way. More and more consumers, however, ask at what price to our health are so many chemicals used in our food production? Although regulations govern the use of these substances, it is rather like testing out video or computer systems, for example, where we are the ultimate guinea pigs in the experiments. Chemicals have been a great help in the history of human development and food production, but it is important that we look to alternatives and have the freedom to choose alternatives. If we worked towards all farming and fruit production in this country to be organic in ten years' time, perhaps this would happen. It might have very important long-term significance to our health.

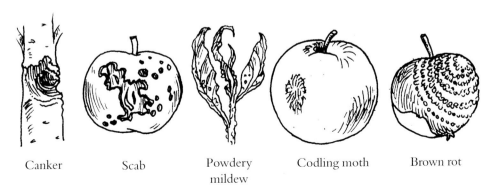

Canker   Scab   Powdery   Codling moth   Brown rot
                              mildew

W E ARE BEGINNING TO DISCOVER MUCH MORE about the origins of our apples thanks to the recent work led in the UK by Dr Barrie Juniper at Oxford. He has published papers on his findings and I particularly like the article about the expeditions to the 'home' of our varieties in Central Asia by Eluned Price in the RHS *Garden*, Volume 126:6, June 2001.

Research on apple taxonomy is also at an exciting stage with the team of Dr Alison Lean and Emma-Jane Lamont, who work for Imperial College at Wye, based at the National Fruit Collections at Brogdale. They are producing accurate descriptions of varieties and the information is being updated on their websites. Brogdale hopes eventually to have information about varieties on its web site. The Imperial College at Wye National Fruit Collection web site has lists of varieties. I strongly recommend reference to the web sites that not only further your knowledge of fruit, but make the National Collections very much open to all.

Emma-Jane Lamont has been very helpful in the preparation of this book. Margaret Burns has also been invaluable with the choice of transparencies from the National Fruit Collection library. We are indebted to all the members of staff who help provide our selections of apples for display and sale at the annual apple weekends as well as for general assistance from Jane Garret, the Director, and Ted Hobday. It was a previous Director, Dr David Pennell, who helped launch the Hertfordshire Orchard Initiative by speaking at its first public meeting. Joan Morgan, a past member of full time staff, edits the Friends of Brogdale Newsletter and over the years I cannot recall an issue that has not taught me something new about the history of fruit or its cultivation. It is easy to join the Friends and your membership will help to preserve our heritage of different types and continue the research on the subject.

Membership of the Royal Horticultural Society is also a 'must' for anyone interested in fruit or gardening in general. Some of the information I required on the Hitchin Pippin was kindly provided and copied by the RHS library at Wisley and they have very well appointed orchards you can enjoy throughout the year.

The next few years should see dramatic advances in our knowledge of apple genetics as well as our ability to accurately identify apples, but already Barrie Juniper's expeditions have transformed our understanding of how we have come to have such an amazingly rich variety of this fruit. Eluned Price describes how Barrie's expeditions to the Ili Valley between Kazakhstan and China, directly north of India and the Himalayas, have allowed us new insights into the possible evolution of the apple types we know today.

We are aware that cross-pollination of famously successful apples continue to help with flavour, disease-free features and prolific production, but the process is not new. In the Field Guide, Chapter 2, I list as much of the origins and cross-breeding we know about, but there has been a continuous natural selection of fruit that has resulted in larger and sweeter varieties as well as the often big, acid cooking ones, too. Barrie's journeys to Tien Shan, (the 'Heavenly Mountains') were made particularly valuable because his Department at Oxford became equipped for accurate DNA comparison work. He was able to go because the Russians and Chinese stopped nuclear testing in the area. Kazahkstan gained independence from the USSR and although the mountains have always been inhospitable, dangerous and disputed territory for visitors from the West, in 1997 Barrie made his first investigations to the north of Afghanistan into Uzbekistan, followed in 1998 by an expedition to the regional capital of Kazakhstan, Alma-Ata (or 'Almaty') which means 'father of apples'. He had found that rather than being derived from different species across Asia or Europe, the various types of apple all appeared to hark back to *Malus sieversii*, known today as *Malus domestica*. This species is a wild form of crab apple that replaces our own wild crab, *Malus sylvestris*, in Central Asia.

Eluned explains that Barrie asked himself: if south central China has the greatest number of different species, how did these turn into the large, red, juicy fruits that we enjoy today? They had originally been small, cherry-sized crabs, propagated through their seeds by birds. (Our word 'crab' for the small, sour apples of the countryside – as distinct from wildings grown by chance from discarded apple cores of popular dessert types – possibly derives from Scandinavian origin: the Swedish for these is *skrabbe*.)

In Kazakhstan his expedition found *M. sieversii* trees growing to their natural size of 9m, much the same height as the standard Bramleys grown in old orchards achieve. This is probably the 'natural' height for most wild apple trees and Barrie found them growing in their hundreds, mixed with pears, apricots, plums and cherries. The apple trees all seemed to be of different sizes and types, from small, yellow crab sorts up to large, red ones, as big as a Howgate Wonder.

They found a match between the *M. sieversii* genetic sequences in their samples and our familiar modern apples. The Russian geneticist, N.I. Vavilov, is thought to have been the first scientist to suggest that *M. sieversii* was the original source of modern cultivars in 1930. The Soviet/Chinese borders were too dangerous even then to visit to carry out further research. It has taken Barrie's field visits and laboratory studies to come up with his guess at the evolution of the modern cultivars. Using the evidence of the twenty *Malus* species in China, which exist in many different forms, he thinks that the small fruit had hard, but edible seeds similar to those of modern rowans. These would have been translocated by birds across the northern hemisphere and our own wild crab apple is descended from these, too.

Around 4.5 million years ago, the Tien Shan mountain range was being squeezed to an even greater height by the movements of the continents and birds continued to transfer seeds into what is now Kazakhstan. Climate change produced deserts such as the nearby Gobi and the apples became cut off in their mountain valleys.

The Ili Valley already included deer, wild boar and bears that would have eaten the autumn fruit drop. Wild horses and donkeys joined them from the Steppes in the west and Barrie feels that these mammals would have selected apples for their juicy sweetness and larger size. Thus these types of fruit evolved with the mammals' constant attention. The pips became bitter with minute amounts of cyanide and their shape developed into a hard, smooth oval shape to pass more easily through the mammalian gut. Human exploitation of the fruit probably developed as tribes followed the animal migration routes (and later 'silk roads' as lines of trade progressed) after the last Ice Age, about 10,000 years ago. We know that grafting and cultivation became widespread around the Mediterranean where evidence of propagation of fruit such as olives and apples exists in early illustrations on pottery and mosaics.

When the bigger, sweeter apples reached Britain it is hard to determine and grafting may have been practised here before the Roman occupation, but Barrie notes that its cultivation in this country ultimately produced 'the finest collection of dessert, culinary and cider fruits ever known'. I expect Barrie will find out as much about other fruits, such as plums and pears, as he has about apples and it all makes for an exciting future in the field of research.

Sources

Brogdale Orchards Limited, Brogdale Road, Faversham, Kent ME13 8XZ (01795 535286 or 01795 535462)

Common Ground, Gold Hill House, 21 High Street, Shaftesbury, Dorset SP7 8JE (01747 850820) www.commonground.org.uk

Royal Horticultural Society, 80 Vincent Square, London SW1P 2PE (020 7834 4333) ; the orchards at Wisley, the RHS Gardens in Surrey are of particular relevance.

There are very good bookshops at Wisley and Brogdale where you can combine visits to the orchards with seeing the best available reference material. They also have very helpful libraries and web sites: www.rhs.org.uk and www.brogdale.org.uk with links to the Wye College Network newsletters and picture galleries.

Hertfordshire Orchard Initiatives c/o Tewin Orchard, Tewin, Welwyn, Herts AL6 0LX

When buying apple trees at general nurseries, look for the 'Trees for Life' label of Frank P. Matthews on the ones you purchase as a good guide to a quality product. These trees are only available through selected independent Garden Centres throughout the UK. To find your local supplier, visit www.trees-for-life.com. Specialist nurseries include Bernwode, Deacon's and Keeper's with contact details listed below.

The Common Ground Book of Orchards (2000)

The *RHS* 'Top Fruit Growing' video is one of the best guides to propagation and care for your trees in their very helpful instructional video series

Ashford, E., *What to do with an Apple* (Elizabeth Ashford)

Baker, H., (1986) *The Fruit Garden Displayed* (London)

Baker, H., (1993) Fruit (Mitchell Beazley, London)

Bernwode Plants Catalogues (Buckinghamshire) www.bernwodeplants.co.uk

Blackburne-Maze, P., (1986) *The Apple Book* (Hamlyn, London)

Brickell, C., (1996) *Pruning & Training* (RHS, London)

Bultitude, J., (1989) *Apples* (Macmillan, London)

Bunyard, E.A., (1920) *A Handbook of Fruits: Apples and Pears* (London)

Crawford, M., (1994) *Directory of Apple Cultivars* (Agroforestry)

Copas, L., (2001) *A Somerset Pomona* (Dovecote Press, Dorset)

Deacon's Nursery Fruit Trees Catalogues deacons.nursery@btopenworld.com

Deal, J., (1985) *Making Cider* (Argus Books, Hemel Hempstead)

Dunn, N., (2001) *Frank P. Matthews Tree Guide for Gardens* Tel. 01584 810214

Garner, R., (1974) *The Grafter's Handbook* (Cassell, London)

Henry Doubleday Research Assoc., (1995) *Fruit & Veg Finder*

Hogg, R., (1878-85) *The Herefordshire Pomona* (Journal of Horticulture, London)

Hogg, R., (2002) *The Fruit Manual* (reprint) (Langford, Wigtown)

Keepers Nursery catalogues, Gallents Court, East Farleigh Kent ME15 0LE Tel. 01622 726465: propagate apple trees from Brogdale Collection to order

Macdonald, B., (1986) *Practical Woody Plant Propagation for Nursery Growers* (Timber Press London)

Morgan, J. and Richards, A. (1993) *The Book of Apples* (Ebury, London)

Popescu, C. (1997). *The Apple Cookbook* (Cavalier, Wiltshire)

Price, E., (2001) article on Dr Barrie Juniper in *Garden* (RHS, 126:6, June)

Proulx, A. & Nichols, L., (1997) *Cider* (Storey, Vermont, USA)

Sanders, R., (1988) *The English Apple* (Phaidon, London)

Taylor, H., (1947) *The Apples of England* (Crosby Lockwood, London)

Williams, R. (Ed), *Cider & Juice Apples* (University of Bristol Printing Unit)

Alphabetical list of apples illustrated

Index